Bhajanamritam

Devotional songs of Sri Mata Amritanandamayi

Volume 2

Mata Amritanandamayi Center
San Ramon, California, United States

Bhajanamritam
Volume 2

Published by:
Mata Amritanandamayi Center
P.O. Box 613
San Ramon, CA 94583-0613
USA

In India:
www.amritapuri.org
inform@amritapuri.org

In USA:
www.amma.org

In Europe:
www.amma-europe.org

Contents

About Pronunciation

The following key is for the guidance of those who are unfamiliar with the transliteration codes of Indian languages which are used in this book.

A	-as	a	in America
AI	-as	ai	in aisle
AU	-as	ow	in how
E	-as	e	in they
I	-as	ea	in heat
O	-as	o	in or
U	-as	u	in suit
KH	-as	kh	in Eckhart
G	-as	g	in give
GH	-as	gh	in loghouse
PH	-as	ph	in shepherd
BH	-as	bh	in clubhouse
TH	-as	th	in lighthouse
DH	-as	dh	in redhead
C	-as	c	in cello
CH	-as	ch-h	in staunch-heart
JH	-as	dge	in hedgehog
Ñ	-as	ny	in canyon
Ś	-as	sh	in shine
Ṣ	-as	c	in efficient
Ṅ	-as	ng	in sing, (nasal sound)
V	-as	v	in valley, but closer to a "w"
ZH	-as	rh	in rhythm

Vowels which have a line on top of them are long vowels, they are pronounced like the vowels listed above but are held for twice the amount of time.

The letters with dots under them (ṭ, ṭh, ḍ, ḍh, ṇ, l, ṣ) are palatal consonants, they are pronounced with the tip of the tongue against the hard palate. Letters without such dots are dental consonants and are pronounced with the tongue against the base of the teeth.

Bhajans

ABHAYAM TAN ARUḶUKA

abhayam tan aruḷuka nīyen
akatāril teḷiyuka kṛṣṇa
anayāttānanda nilāvāyi
teḷi mānam nalkuka hṛttil

Give me refuge, O Krishna, and appear within me. Be the unwaning full moon and shine in the clear sky of my heart.

paramārtha poruḷē, nīyen
paritāpa kanalaṇayānāyi
kanivin amṛtam pozhiyikkū
paricil ñān kandu tozhaṭṭe

Thou, Who art the Quintessence of Truth, please shower the ambrosia of Grace to quench the embers of my grief. Please let me have Thy vision and offer my salutations to Thee without delay.

kāṭāke kūriruḷāyi
kūṭārum kūṭṭinumillā
kāruṅya kaṭalallē nī
kāruṇyam tūkukayillē?

The forest is becoming dark and there is none for company. Art Thou not the ocean of compassion? Won't Thou shower Thy Grace?

snēhattin tiri nāḷatte
nīḷattil nīṭṭuka kṛṣṇa
kāṇaṭṭe kaṇi kāṇaṭṭe
cēṇuttā padatār pūkkaḷ

Pull out the wick of the lamp of love, O Krishna, and let me behold those beautiful flower-like Feet.

ABHAYATTINĪMAKAN

abhayattinīmakan aviratam tirayunnu
atirattu kēzhunnu ñān ammē
agati ñān avirāmam tirayunnu dēvi nin
anaśvara mahimāvil uyarttukenne

O Mother, this son is weeping and incessantly seeking Your shelter. I who have no other path, O Devi, pray that You raise me in Your immortal greatness. I pray, raise me in Your immortal greatness.

ālambahīnan ñān tēṭunnu daivamē [ambikē]
ātanka mukti tannīṭāttatentu nī?
ārādhanā puṣpam vāṭunnatin munpē
svīkarikkyuvān nī varillē ammē
svīkarikkyuvān nī varillē

O God, I have no other support. Won't You release me from this sorrow? Won't You come to accept this flower (my mind) which is an offering for worship, won't You come to accept this flower?

pāricha śōkattinnazhattilāzhūvān
nī niyōgikkumennī makanōrttīllā
nin nāmamen nāvil ninnakannīlallo
nin prēma tīrttham pozhikkāttatentahō ammē
nin prēma tīrttham pozhikkāttatentahō

This grief is ever increasing; I never thought that You would place me in such a situation. Your name has not vanished from my lips; won't You pour Your holy offering of love; O Mother, why don't You pour Your holy offering?

ABHĪSHṬA VARADĀYIKĒ

abhīṣṭa varadāyikē
jñāna sukha dāyikē
janma phala dāyikē varū
hṛdayattil kuṭi koḷḷum kamalāmbikē

O Kamalambike (Divine Mother), Bestower of all desired boons, Giver of Supreme Knowledge, Arbiter of my destiny, come, let me welcome You, Indweller of my heart.

ōrmakaḷ taḷiriṭṭa nāḷ mutal ñān ninte
ārādhanā puṣpamāyirunnu
ōrāyiram bhāva gītangaḷāl ninne
ātmāvil tētukayāyirunnu
manam ārdramāy tīruka āyirunnu

Right from the earliest days, as far back as my memory takes me, I felt that I was the flower that was offered for Your worship. I looked for You in the depths of my soul by singing a thousand hymns of devotion, and my mind became totally immersed in You.

hṛdayam piṭayunna bhakti bhāvēśa pātayil
ēkānta pathikayāy ñān
ōrō malarilum ōrō mukililum
viriyunna nin mukham nōkki ninnu — ammē
enne maṛannu ñān nōkki ninnu

I was a lonely traveller on the ecstatic path of bhakti, and my heart blossomed. I saw Your face in each flower that my eyes took in, in each leaf, and I stood there wonder-struck, totally oblivious of anything else in the Universe.

ĀDI ŚAKTI MAHĀ LAYAMKARI

ādi śakti mahā layamkari
nitya śānti sandāyinī
kāli kāli sanātanī
amṛtānandamayi bhairavī

O Primordial Power, the Eternal One, Kali, Who brings all phenomena to their conclusion and merges them with the One Source, Bestower of perpetual peace, Bhairavi, (Consort of Bhairava, i.e., Shiva) Whose nature is immortal bliss.

satyamāy śiva rūpamāy
śubha nitya sundara sāramāy
etra kalpangaḷāyi rasippu nī
śāśvatē durgē kai tozhām (ādi śakti)

O Durga, the timelessly existing One, how many aeons have You been watching this world-play in delight, while remaining as the auspicious, non-changing Pure Essence, the beautiful underlying Reality? I fold my hands in salutation to You.

ninna bhaumamī sarga kēḷiyil
nī rasichu madikkavē
khinnarāyi kēṇu vāṇiṭunnōre
kai piṭichu karēttanē (ādi śakti)

While You revel in Your own pristine plane of existence, far removed from the afflictions of this earthly plane, please do offer a helping hand to the multitudes here, who desperately need to be rescued and taken to a safe shore.

ennu kāṇum ñān ennu kāṇum ñān
ente jīvanām ammaye?
ennu kāṇum ñān sarva sākṣiyām
ente unmayām ammaye? (ādi śakti)

O, when will I ever see my Mother, when will I ever see the Witness of all, my very Life, my only Reality — my Mother?

nirguṇa saguṇātmaka
brahma rūpiṇī bhavatārinī
nin kṛpā lēśa monninās kṣaṇam
rakṣayārkku labhichiṭām (ādi śakti)

O Mother, my sole means to cross the ocean of transmigration, You are verily Brahman, the Absolute, essentially formless, but also capable of manifesting many forms. Just an iota of Your Grace is enough to immediately bring about the salvation of anyone.

īkṣaṇam nī nalkiṭeṇam sudha
nirmala prēma bhaktiye
ninte bhaktiyil mungiyāndu
nin pāda tāriṇa pūkaṇē (ādi śakti)

Please grant me pure, taintless love and devotion this very moment. All I want is to immerse myself in devotion and attain Your holy Feet.

AKHILA LŌKA NĀYAKĪ

akhila lōka nāyakī
ambā ārthi nāśinī

O Queen of all the worlds, You are the Destroyer of desires.

saguṇa viguṇa rūpiṇī
sakala durita vāriṇī

You are with and without attributes, Your form removes all sorrows.

nikhila bhūvana mōhinī
nigama āgama bhōdhinī

Enchantress of all the worlds, Instructor of the Scriptures.

cira śubha sukha dāyini
manasi lasatu pāvanī

Always sacred, Giver of happiness, reside in my mind, O Embodiment of purity.

nirātiśayānandini
nirupama guṇa śālinī

Blissful one, You Whose attributes are incomparable,

srita jana pari pālinī
manasi lasatu pāvanī

O Protectress of seekers, Embodiment of purity, reside in my mind.

ALLĀH TUMAHO

allāh tumaho īśvara tumaho
tumi hō rāma rahīm (2x)
yesu tumaho nānaka tumaho
zoroastrabhi hō mahavīra tumaho
gautama buddha karīm (2x)
mērē rām mērē rām rāma rahīm (3x)

You are Allah and Ishwara;
You are Rama and Rahim.
You are Jesus and Guru Nanak;
You are Zoroastra, Mahavira and Gautama Buddha.
O my Rama, O my Rama, Rama Rahim.

AMALA PRAKĀŚAMĒ

amala prakāśamē arikilanaññiṭān
avadhikaḷ entinu nīṭṭunnu nī
alayunnu nin putri (an)
aviṭutte darśikkān
azhal tingi ninniṭum bhūvilūṭe

O Immaculate Light, who do You keep on postponing my coming close to You? Your daughter (son) is wandering through the world swarming with sorrows just for the sight of You.

karaḷ tiṅgum vēdana cumalēri pāritil
karuṇā rasattine tēṭiṭunnu
hṛdaya śrī kōvilin mani viḷakkām ammē
kazhivillā paital ñān kēṇiṭunnū

Carrying the burden of an aching heart on my shoulders, I wander through the world in search of the nectar of compassion. Mother, You who are the lamp in the inner sanctum of my heart, this helpless child is crying for You.

nitya prakāśamē nīṛum manōvyatha
nīkkiṭān ettumō en jananī
nī tanne yennuṭe sarvavum mātāvē
nī tanne lōkattin ādhāravum

The Light Eternal, my Mother, will You come to expel the pain of my heart? O Mother, You are also the substratum of the world.

AMBĀ PARAMĒŚVARI

ambā paramēśvari akhilāṇḍēśvari
ādi parā śakti pālaya mām

O Supreme Mother Goddess, Empress of the Universe, the Primal Supreme Energy, save me!

śrī bhuvanēśvari rāja rājēśvari
ānanda rūpiṇi pālaya mām
amṛtānanda rūpini pālaya mām
amba paramēśvari akhilāndēśvari
ādi parā śakti pālaya mām
śrī bhuvanēśvari rāja rājēśvari
ānandamāyi mā pālaya mām
amṛtānanda mayi mā
pālaya mām

O Ruler of the Earth, Ruler of rulers, Whose form is Bliss, protect me! Protect me, O Amritanandamayi. O Supreme Mother Goddess, Empress of the Universe, the Primal Supreme Energy, protect me! O Blissful One, protect me!

AMBĒ PĀHIMĀM

ambē pāhimām jagadambē pāhimām
sarva mangaḷayāmen ambē pāhimām

O Mother, protect me, O Mother of the Universe, protect me. Protect me, O Mother, Who is all-auspicious.

ammē nin vātsalyam nukarunna samayam
amṛtānanda mayam hṛdayam
kanivōde ñangaḷe ammē nī tazhukumbōḷ
kuḷir candanattin layam manassil

When I enjoy Your motherly affection, there is an abundance of nectarous bliss in my heart. O Mother, Your caress, full of kindness, is like the cooling sandalwood paste.

aśru bindu kaḷām pūkkaḷumāyi varum
arumakkiṭāngale kānumbōḷ
ammē nin mizhikalum niṛaññu tuḷumbunnu
aśaranaril kṛpa coriyunnū

When You see Your beloved children come to You with flowers of tears, Mother, Your eyes also fill and overflow with tears, showering kindness on those who have no other refuge.

āpāda madhuram nin nāma saṅkīrtanam
aviśmaraṇīyam ammē - tava bhāva darśanam
apāra samsāra sāgaram māyunnu
akatāril teḷiyunnu nin sannidhānam

To hear the chanting of Your Divine Name is sweet. Your Divine Mood is unforgettable. Then, the endless ocean of transmigration ceases to exist, and Your presence becomes clearly felt in my heart.

AMBIKĒ ENNANTARANG

ambikē ennantarangē viḷangunna
sundara surabhila nimiṣangaḷil
ānandābdhiyil ūḷiyiṭṭūḷiyiṭṭu
ākave unmattayākum ñān
ākave unmattayākum ñān

Goddess Ambika shining in my heart, I will become intoxicated. Immersed in bliss during those beautiful and rare moments and diving deep into happiness, I will become completely intoxicated.

attiru cintāsaraṇiyilpeṭṭu
ī lōka bhōgangaḷellām
pāṭē maṛannū paṛannu paṛannu nin
pādē layikkum ñān

Traversing the sacred lane of Your memory, I will forget all worldly pleasures. Then I will fly to greater heights and merge into Your Holy Feet.

AMMA TANNĀ MAṬI TAṬṬIL

amma tannā maṭi taṭṭil paṛannettān
sad gurō nī ciṛa kēkukillē

O Satguru, won't You give me wings so that I can fly over to the wondrous lap of my Mother?

rāveriññīṭunnu
rāppāṭi māzhkunnu
ñān uṛangāte karaññiṭunnu

It is almost day-break, the night-owl is still hooting and I have been awake all night crying for my Mother.

makkaḷ tan pāpa viṣam vizhuṅgum tyāga
ganga tan tīrtthattil ennaṇayum?

When will I merge with the holy waters of the Ganga, which remain pure even after being sullied by the deadly sins of Her children?

ventu nīṛunna
varkkakṣaṇam āsvāsam
nalkīṭum ammaye ennu kāṇum

When will I see the Mother who gives instant relief to all those smouldering inside with undissipated passions?

ammē dayāmayī collu collinnu ñān
eṅgane ammayil vannu cērum

O Mother, Compassion Incarnate, tell me, tell me today — how will I become one with You, Mother?

nāmam cirakākki dhyānam cirakākki
prēma vyōmattil uyarnnīṭānō?

May I take off on that aerial vehicle called Love — may I use the repetition of Thy Holy Name as one of its wings and meditation as the other.

kāma koṭuṅkāttu cīṛiyaṭikkunnu
krōdha miṭiveṭṭi minniṭunnu

The gusty winds of desire are howling around me. Bursts of anger flare up like lightning and thunder.

mōha karim kūriruṭṭi luṭengane
dūra dūram parannettiṭum ñān

How will I cover all that distance on my two wings through the inky darkness of delusion?

enni lūṭen cidākāśattilēkku ñān
ūḷiyiṭṭūrnnu parannīṭaṭṭe

Let me fly through my inner skies, and soar up to those heights of pure consciousness.

ā vyōma vistāra tīrattengō amma
darśanam nalkum kalari undu

Somewhere is that lofty expanse — there is the temple where my Mother sits, giving darshan.

AMMĀ TĀYĒ JAGANMĀTĀ

ammā tāyē jaganmātā ammā tāyē jaganmāyē
untan karunai tēṭi vantēn
entan kavalai akala kandēn
ammā amṛtānandamayi tāyē tāyē amṛtānandamayi

O Mother, You are the Mother of the universe. O Mother, You are the Mother of the world of illusion. I came in search of Your compassion, and watched my sorrows wither away.

tara vēndum eppozhutum un pārvai enakku
vara vēndum eppozhuthum un ninaivē enakku
kōṭi poruḷum īṭal un malaraṭikku
vāzhkkāyin poruḷ tanta tāyē nī enakku

May You always bestow Your attention on me; may I always unceasingly remember You. Abundant wealth is not equal to Your holy feet. You have shown me the purpose of this life, O Mother.

nīyalla tillai śeyal ellām ulakil
nān enṭre eṇṇam vaḷarāmal manatil
nan nalam illāmal paṇiyātta nal
varamaruḷa vēndum ammā nī enakku

There is no other doer than You in this world. Let not the "I" consciousness grow in my mind. Without expecting the results of action, O Mother, give me the boon of working for You.

arivilla enakku jñāna mozhi tantu
azhiyum poruḷai uṇaravi śeytu
azhivillā ānanda poruḷai kāṭṭi
āṟutal tara vēndum tāyē nī enakku

Give this ignorant one the wisdom of knowledge and make me understand what is the nature of the transient. By revealing the changeless Essence of eternal happiness, O Mother, give me the nectar of Eternal Bliss.

AMMĒ AMMĒ

ammē ammē ammē ammē
ennātma sangītamē
ammē nin kuññine rakṣichu koḷḷuvān
vaikunnatentē param poruḷe
kēṇu kēṇīvana vīthiyil ambikē
vīṇu kiṭakkanō ennumennum

O Mother, O Mother, O Mother, O Mother, that song from the soul. O Mother Divine, Why are You delaying to save Your child? Am I supposed to suffer in this mundane world forever? Weeping and crying, no end in sight.

jīvitam tannu nī vāsana tannu nī

nīṛumī māyayil taḷḷi enne
kālam kazhiyunnu jīvan eriyunnu
kandatillammaye mātraminnum (ammē ammē)

You have given me my life, You have given me my desires, and You pushed me into this burning illusory world. Time goes forward and life continues painfully. But alas! I have not yet seen my Mother!

ninnē varuttiṭān ententum ceytiṭām
innē veṭiññiṭām entu mentum
kaṇṇīr coriññu hṛtkkaṇṇē viḷippu ñān
maṇṇinum viṇṇinum ammē ammē (ammē ammē)

I will do anything, be it the hardest thing I am asked; I will renounce anything, be it my dearest, this very day — just to get You to come to me. My inner eye, the eye within my heart, sheds tears, and cries out to the earth and the sky, "O Mother, O Mother!"

AMMĒ AMṚTĀNANDAMAYĪ

ammē amṛtānandamayī dēvī anugrahikkū
ivane anugrahikkū
ajñānam naśikkān ānandam kaivarān
anugrahikkū dēvī nī anugrahikkū

O Mother Amritanandamayi Devi, bless me, do bless me. So that my ignorance may be destroyed and I may come to experience bliss, bless me Devi, bless me.

mayāndhakārattil varzhitēdi alayumī
ezhayām ennil kaniyū dēvī nī anugrahikkū
ārōrum illāte pāpa bhāravumentī
alayunnu ñān dēvī nī anugrahikkū

O Devi, be compassionate and bless this helpless one, who searches in vain for the way through the darkness of cosmic delusion. With a burden of sins, I am wandering helplessly. I have nobody. O Devi, please bless me.

nin divya darśanam ēkī nīyennil ammē
karuṇa mazha coriyū dēvī nī anugrahikkū
ā divya divyangaḷam nimiṣaṅgal kāttu
tapassu ceyyum ñān dēvi nī anugrahikkū
nī anugrahikkū

Grant me the vision of Thy Divine Form, O Mother, shower thy compassion on me and bless me, O Devi. Waiting for that blissful moment (of seeing Thy Divine Form), I remain constantly in meditation, O Devi, please bless me.

AMME AMṚTĀNANDAMAYI SARVĀGAMA

ammē amṛtānandamayī
sarvāgama mantramayī
ammē viśva prēma mayī
vandē mātā praṇavamayī

O Mother Amritanandamayi, one who sings all the scriptures through Your words, O Mother, You are the most loving Universal Mother. Salutations to You, the embodiment of Pranava (OM).

anupamamamme nin tiru mizhikaliḷ
ozhukum karuṇā rasa laharī
anupadam ammē! nin tiru mozhikaliḷ
aliyān en karaluzharī (ammē)

The nectar of compassion that flows from Your face is beyond comparison. At each step, my heart wishes only to dissolve into Your sweet words.

aṛiyillamme! engane en karal
atiyaravāyī nin kazhaliḷ
ala katal poleyapāra kṛpāmṛtam
ozhukum nin tiru natayil (ammē)

I do not know, my Mother, how my mind sought refuge as a slave at Your holy feet. Incessant nectar of compassion flows like the sea full of waves from Your holy abode.

AMMĒ YĪ JĪVENDE

ammē yī jīvente
kaṇṇunīr oppuvān
ammē yī jīvannu śānti nalkān
ammē jaganmayī aṅgallā tillārum
nin pādalābha māṇātma lābham

O Mother of the Universe, there is no one other than You who can wipe the tears off this face, who can liberate this soul. Coming to Your feet, this soul realizes itself.

kaṣṭam! manassinnum lakṣyattilettāte
dukhi cuzhalunnu māyayālē
niṣkāma bhakti yōṭe eppōzhum nin kazhal
keṭṭippuṇarān anugrahikkū

Alas! This mind is even now wallowing in sorrow having lost its way in Maya before finding its Goal. Please bless me that I shall forever hold You in a tight embrace with pure devotion.

ghōra samsāra mahārnavam tannil nin
pādāravindam āṇenabhayam
nīṛi pukayumenn ātmavil ittiri
snēhāmṛtam tūkān nī varillē?

In this fearsome ocean of birth and death, the only refuge is Your Lotus Feet. Won't You come and sprinkle a little of the nectar of Love on this smouldering self?

kāṇi nēram kalaññīṭāte nin kazhal
cinta ceyyunnōrī pinchu kuññīl
kāla viḷambam varāte en amma nī
cārattaṇaññātma śānti nalkū

This little infant spends every single moment meditating on Your form. Please do not keep me waiting any more — draw me close to You and bestow inner tranquility to this tortured soul.

AMṚTAMAYI ĀNANDAMAYI

amṛtamayi ānandamayi amṛtānandamayī
amṛtamayi ānandamayi amṛtānandamayī
ammē amṛtānandamayī

O Goddess of nectar, Goddess of immortal bliss, O Mother Amritanandamayi, O Goddess of nectar, Goddess of eternal bliss.

maruvuka māmaka mānasa tāril
marataka maṇi varṇṇē
aṭiyanorāśrayam ennum ninnuṭe
caraṇāmbujam ammē

Come and dwell in my heart, You who have the hue of the emerald gem. The sole refuge for this poor man is always Your lotus feet.

kaṇṇinu kaṇṇāyi uḷḷil viḷangum
kaṇṇanum ammē nī
sarvva jagattinu mātāvām
jagadambayum ammē nī

You who shine forth from within as the inner eye for the external eye, You are also the Mother of Kanna. You are the Mother of this whole Universe, You are the Goddess of this Universe.

karayum makkaṭe kaṇṇīr kaṇḍāl
karaḷ aliyunnavaḷē
kanivām pālu koṭuttu talōṭum
karuṇāmayiyammē

O Mother, on seeing Your children shed tears Your heart melts with concern. On feeding Your children with the milk of tenderness You lovingly caress them, O compassionate Mother.

tāvaka pāda sarōjamiha pūjanam
mānasa paramānandam
mātāvē nin makanāmivane
kaiveṭi arutamme

Offering worship at Your lotus feet gives infinite bliss to one's mind. O Mother, please do not forsake this child of Yours.

AMṚTĀNANDAMAYĪ AMMĀ

amṛtānandamayī ammā amṛtānandamayī
umaye mūkāmbikayē
mūvulakin nāyakiyē
uṇmaye tann uṇmaye
veṇmayāl maṛaitavaḷe
uyirāna uyirkaḷellām stutippavaḷe ammā nī
uṛavōṭu kāpāttu uṭal
edutu vantavaḷe

Umaye Mookambikaye, the Empress of the three worlds, hiding Truth, Thy Truth, beyond the white veil. All living things worship Thee, Amma! Save me by binding me unto Thee, O Devi Incarnate.

ammā ammā ammā
uṇmai tēdi tēdi ulakellām nān alainten
ulakellām payanam śeytum uṇmaye kāṇavillai
uṇmai kāṇa alainta nān unniṭattil vantai ammā
uṛavōṭu kāppāttu uṇmaikkāṭṭa vēndum ammā

Searching for Truth, I roamed all over the world. But even after seeking all over the world, I still did not find the Truth. Searching for Truth, I came to Thee, Amma. Save me by binding me unto Thee, and show me the Truth, Amma!

ammā ammā ammā
ulakam un anbukkāga
pichai kēkkut ammā
unnai kāna mūvūlakum
tuṭiyāi tuṭikutammā
un caraṇam vaṇaṅkiṭa ulakellām kotikkut ammā
uḷḷurukki anbukkāṭṭa tāmatam vēndā ammā

The world is begging for Thy love. Seeking Thy Vision, the three worlds are in agony, Amma! The world is burning, pining to worship Thy Feet. Don't delay—melt with compassion and reveal Thy Love.

AMṚTĀNANDAMAYĪ JANANI

amṛtānandamayī janani
karuṇāmayī nī kṛpāmayī nī
vijñānamayī ānandamayī ammā
amṛtānandamayī

Mother Amritanandamayi, Thou art the embodiment of mercy, of compassion, of wisdom, and of bliss.

vijña vināśini vināyaka janani
divya mayī amma vidyāmayi
buddhi pradāyini vēda svarūpiṇi
bōdhamayī amma
satcinmayī amma
amṛtānandamayī

Thou art the remover of all obstacles, Thou, Who art the mother of Vinayaka Ganesha. Mother, Thou art the embodiment of holiness, of knowledge. Thou art the Bestower of intellect. Vedas are Thy form. Thou art the conscious and Pure Self, O, Mother Amritanandamayi.

pustaka dhāriṇi vīnāpāni
brahma svarūpiṇi sarasvati
dēvi mahālakṣmi pārvati śaṅkari
ādi parāśakti jagadambikē amma
amṛtānandamayī

Amritanandamayi, Thou art Saraswati, Goddess of Knowledge, holding the book and veena in Her hands. Thou art Brahman Itself. Thou art Mahalakshmi, Goddess of Wealth, Parvati, Goddess of Power, Sankari, the Auspicious One, and Adi Para Sakti, the Primordial Power.

brahmamayī amma viṣnumayī
śaktimayī śiva śaktimayī
śrī kṛṣṇa bhāvamāyī
parāśakti bhāvamāyī
kāttaruleṇam jagadambikē amma
amṛtānandamayī

Thou art Vishnumayi the dynamic Power of the Sustainer and Shiva-Shakti the Passive and Active aspects. Mother of the Universe, please protect us by adopting the Krishna Bhava and Devi Bhava, O, Amritanandamayi.

AMṚTĀNANDAMAYĪ JAY JAY

amṛtānandamayī jay jay
sad guru rūpiṇi mā
mangaḷa kāriṇi mā
vandē karuṇā nirjhari mā (amṛta)

Victory! Victory to Mother Amritanandamayi who is embodied as Guru. Salutations to Mother who is the bestower of auspiciousness and who is the ever-flowing stream of Grace.

prēma tarangiṇi mā jai jai
vimala suhāsini mā
subhāvaraṇa lasē vandē
jyōti sukēśini mā (amṛta)

Victory! Victory to Mother, who creates waves of love with an untainted smile, who shines in white garments. Salutations to Mother, respendent with adorable hair.

satya svarūpiṇi mā jai jai
nitya nirañjini mā
śakti mahēśvari mā vandē
bhakti rasōnmanī mā (amṛta)

Victory, victory to Mother, the Embodiment of Truth, the Eternal Unifier. Salutations to Mother, the Great Goddess Shakti, the Bliss of Divine Love.

karma vidhāyini mā nityam
adharma vibhañjini mā
jagadōdhāriṇi mā vandē
jagad sañcālini mā

O Bestower of the fruits of action, the eternal Destroyer of unrighteousness. Salutations to the Uplifter of the world, the One Who moves throughout the Universe.

sadguru jñānamayī jai jai
tyāga nidarśini mā
dukha vimōcini mā vandē
sadgati dāyini mā

Victory, victory to Mother, the Master of Knowledge, Who demonstrates real renunciation. Salutations Mother, the Destroyer of Sorrow, Who bestows the Goal of life.

AMṚTĀNANDAMAYI MĀ TUCCH KŌ

amṛtānandamayi mā tucch kō lākhō praṇām
lākhō praṇām tucch kō kōṭi praṇām

O Mother Amritanandamayi, millions of prostrations to You, millions of prostrations to You!

jai jai sarasvati mātā tucch kō lākhō praṇām
lākhō praṇām tucch kō kōṭi praṇām

Victory, victory to Mother Saraswati, Goddess of Divine Knowledge. Millions of prostrations to You, millions of prostrations to You!

jai jai lakṣmi mātā tucch kō lākhō praṇām
lākhō praṇām tucch kō kōṭi praṇām

Victory, victory to Mother Lakshmi, Goddess of wealth and prosperity. Millions of prostrations to You, millions of prostrations to You!

jai santōṣi mayyā tucch kō lākho praṇām
lākhō praṇām tucch kō kōṭi praṇām

Victory to Mother Santoshi! Millions of prostrations to You, millions of prostrations to You!

gōvārdhana giridhāri tucch kō lākho praṇām
lākhō praṇām tucch kō kōṭi praṇām
śata kōṭi praṇām

Millions of prostrations to Sri Krishna Who lifted the Govardhana mountain. Millions of prostrations to You, millions of prostrations to You!

AMṚTĀNANDAMAYĪ SADGURU

amṛtānandamayī sadguru mama jananī
mama manō rañjinī bhava bhaya bhañjinī
amṛtānandamayī

Amritanandamayi is my Satguru and Mother. She is the One who delights my mind and annihilates all fears caused by worldliness.

kaṭal ōḷangaḷ pōl duritaṅgaḷ
amṛtānandamayī
aruḷvāyi mama jananī
aśaraṇanivanāyi
tava pada malarina
tuṇayāyi mama jananī

Disasters are always coming up, one after another, like waves of the sea. O Mother Amritanandamayi, please let Your two Lotus Feet be the constant companions of this helpless one.

alayum kaliyin veyilil ivaniha
amṛtānandamayī taṇalāyi mama jananī
iruḷ potiyum mama matiyil
arivin oḷiyāyi mama jananī

While this one wanders in the scorching noon-day sun of the Kali Yuga, O Mother Amritanandamayi, You are my shade. To my mind enveloped in darkness, You are the beacon of Light.

AMṚTAPURĒŚVARI DĒVĪ

amṛtapurēśvari dēvī dayāmayī
tava caraṇam śrithajana śaraṇam
anupamam amba; tavamala jīvitam
aka mukham āyaṛivōrk akhilam

O Ruler of Amritapuri, Devi, who is the Abundance of kindness, Your Feet become the refuge of those who surrender to You. Unique is Your pure life, which is the source of knowledge for the inwardly drawn.

puḷakitham amba tavasmaraṇam hṛdi
tava naṭanōtsava bhāvarasam
kuḷir mizhi nīril viṭarnna japāñjali
malarukaḷ tāvaka pādasaram

Mother, remembrance of You causes my hair to stand on end and my heart is filled with the divine mood of Your dance. Your anklets are the flowers which bloom in the coolness of teardrops, and which are offered to You in worship.

tava tiru cēvaṭi kūppuvatengane
akṛtikaḷ uḷḷu ṇarāta janam
avarilum amba! kṛpā madhu tūki
anugraham ēkuvatā hṛdayam

How can those who have not done virtuous deeds, whose inner mind is not awakened, ever prostrate at Your Holy Feet? But Your heart is so compassionate that You indeed shower Your Grace on them and bless them.

aṇiyaṇiyāy anuvāsaram ākula
karma śataṇgaḷil uḷḷurukī
priya sutaramba tavānghrikaḷil
bhava - bhāram ozhichu
ramippu sukham

Every day the endless stream of various actions causes sorrow and a painful heart. Mother, Your darling children come and ease the burden of worldly life at Your feet and enjoy happiness.

curulala pōle samṛdhiyezhum nija
karimukil vēṇi maṛachu sadā
paṇimati, veṇmukil cuzhnnoḷi vīsi
vaṭiviyalunna mukhāmburuham

Like dark rain clouds, Your abundant, wavy locks of hair hide Your face. Your lotus face shines like the full moon encircled by the clouds.

kanivozhukum mizhi mañju mṛdusmita
mamṛtoḷi vāṅgmadhu māsmaramām
kara parilāḷana cumbana ātmana
kalavikaḷ amba vimōhanamām

Your merciful glance and sweet smile, Your words like nectar and honey are all mesmerizing. Your caresses, kisses and sportings, O Mother, are enchanting.

eḷimayil eḷima pakarnnoru śikṣaṇa
dakṣatayāl nija siṣya gaṇam
tavapādarēnu aṇiññu munīśvara
padavi varichuyarunnaniśam

Through Your efficient training, Your disciples are taught to be humbler than the humblest. They wear the dust of Your Feet and grow to the level of great sages day by day.

bharata janitri munīndra kula prasu
vulakitilenna viśeṣa padam
amṛtapurēśvari sārthakamay
tava tiru avatāra kathā sudhayāl

The old adage that India is the Mother of saints and sages on earth becomes true, O Amritesvari, by the ambrosial stories of Your divine incarnation.

dhanamada tṛṣṇa muzhuttu timarttu
puḷaykkumiṭattilatāsakalam
kanavu kaṇakku veṭiññuyuvōṣmaḷa
hṛdaya śataṅgaḷ tavārchakarāy

In this place where the rich become haughty, all is renounced like the visage of a dream by hundreds of warm, youthful hearts of those who become Your worshippers.

mahiyil mahēśvara pūja janāvana
tāpamatiluḷḷu kulirttu dṛḍham
aha mozhivākki anaśvarar ākuvat
amṛtapurēśvari tan niyamam

To become immortal, on this earth, for the people in general, worship of Shiva and penance by which the mind is saturated and made firm, thus removing the ego, is the rule established by Amritapuresvari (Mother).

hṛdaya malarkkaṇi vechu vaṇaṅgiya
mōgha kṛtārtthata nēṭiyavar
diśi diśi tāvaka kīrtti paratti
udikkukayāy nava satya yugam

By surrendering the flower of the heart, those whose lives have become pure and fulfilled, spread Your glories to all quarters and thus bring about a new Satya Yuga (the age of Truth, the Golden Age).

AMṚTAVARṢIṆI

amṛtavarṣiṇi ammē harṣakāriṇi
atula śālinī ammē bhuvanamōhini
mṛdula bhāshiṇi ammē mauna bhāṣiṇi
triguṇa kāriṇi ammē hṛdayahāriṇi

Amma, You are constantly showering nectar on us. You are the source of eternal bliss. You are unequalled in Your prowess and You constantly delude the world with Your Maya. You are soft spoken and at the same time You speak and teach in silence. You are the source of the three gunas (qualities of Nature). Amma, You steal our hearts.

tripura sundari ammē tribhuvanēśvari
hṛdivihāriṇi ammē triśūladhārini
abhayadāyini ammē amaravāhini
bhavabhayāpahē ammē pāhimāmbikē

Amma, You are the Queen of all the three worlds and most beautiful. You are always playing in our hearts. You sport a trident and provide us with refuge from all fear and calamities. Gods are always worshipping You. Protect us, O Devi Who removes the fear of birth and death.

bhuvanamōhanam ammē tāvakānanam
kalivināṣanam ammē nin prakīrttanam
bhavadanugraham ammē bhavatu pratyaham
manasi sarvadā ammē lasatu nin padam

Your form is bewitching to behold and gladdens the heart. Singing Your glory and praise destroys the sins of the Kali age. The gods praise Your greatness and You are Immortal Bliss. You destroy our desires and Your lotus feet are our eternal treasure.

karaḷinutsavam ammē tava jayōtsavam
kavana mōhanam ammē tava kathāmṛtam
sujana nandinī ammē sukrita rañjinī
amṛtavāhinī ammē amarasēvini

Hearing stories of Your victory is a festival for my mind. Enchanting are their nectar-like qualities. O Amma, You are nectar and the gods constantly worship You, the Protector and Enchantress of those of good deeds.

natajanāvalī ammē suma bharāñjalī
ayi mahēśvarī ammē ārti hārinī
kṛta yugōdayam ammē tāva kōdayam
tava padāmbujam ammē nikhila kāmadam

O Mahesvari, Destroyer of avarice, worshipping You with folded palms is the only recourse for the denizens of this world. Your lotus feet are the bestowers of all desires.

AMUTAM POZHIYUM

amutam pozhiyum ānanda rūpiṇi
amṛtānandamayi ammā amṛtānandamayi
idaya malaril amṛtam pozhivāye
amṛtānandamayī ammā

O Mother Amritanandamayi, embodiment of bliss, kindly shower the nectar of immortality in my heart.

praṇava poruḷāyi viḷankum tāyē
un tāmarai pādamē śaraṇam
taḷarum enakku nizhal tarum karpagamē
un pādame enakku śaraṇam

You shine as OM. You offer shelter as the wish-fulfilling tree to those weary of the worldly life. I take refuge at Your lotus feet.

muzhukum enakku kalamāyi varuvāyi
piṛaviyai aṛuttu viṭutalai taruvāyi
eṅkaḷ manatil enṭrum oḷirvāyi

untan uṇarvvinai entrum taruvāyi

I'm drowning in this ocean of worldly existence. Please rescue me and ferry me across. Kindly liberate me, cutting asunder the chain of birth and death. May I ever be aware of Your effulgent Presence in my heart.

ANĀTHANĀKKARUTĒ

anāthanākkarutē ivane sanātanī lalitē
anāthanākkarutē ivane sanātanī lalitē
anātharaśaraṇar tiṅgumī bhuvanam
nitānta dukha vihāram

O Lalita (an aspect of Devi), don't leave me as an orphan. The world teeming with destitutes and orphans is ever the abode of sorrow.

naṟumaṇam utirum malarukaḷanavadhi
vilasunnu nin mānasa vāṭiyil
kozhuyunnorī pūvin vēdana
aṟiyunnuvō nī hṛdayēśvarī

There are many sweet scented flowers in the garden of Your mind. O sovereign of my heart, are You aware of the grief of this withering flower?

tava caraṇāmbujam abhayam tēṭi
kanavukaḷ pōlētra varṣangaḷ maraññu
kaniññatillinnum karuṇāmayī ambā
coriyuvatennō nin kṛpā kaṭākṣam

How many years have vanished in vain like a dream in search of Your Lotus Feet for refuge? The compassionate Mother has not yet shown mercy. When is She going to lavish Her graceful glance on me?

ANĀDINIDHANĒ

anādinidhanē anupamacaritē
amṛitānandamayī matē [amara vidhāyini mātē]
akaluṣa hṛdaya vihāriṇi ramaṇī
akhila carācara jananī

śive śivapare śivamayacaritē
śiva mana nilayē śubhadē
śruti pada naṭana manōhara caraṇe
śaraṇāgata jana varadē

harihara sahitē surajanavinutē
parasukha vitarana niratē
madhumaya mṛduhasitānana mahitē
manalaya dāyini lalitē

kuvalaya nayanē kisalaya caraṇē
natajana pālana hṛdayē
vikasita kamala sukōmala vadanē
bhava bhaya śamane vandē

anādinidhanē	The beginningless Destroyer
anupamacaritē	One who has an incomparable story
amaravidhāyini	The ordainer of deathlessness
mātē	O Mother
akaluṣahṛdaya vihariṇi	One who sports in a calm heart
ramaṇi	One who gives loving delight
akhila caracara janani	The Mother of all moving and unmoving things
śivē	Auspicious one
śivaparē	One who is superior even to Lord Shiva

śivamayacaritē	One whose antecedents are auspicious
śivamananilayē	One whose abode is Shiva's heart
śubhadē	The bestower of auspiciousness
śrutipadanadana manōhara caraṇē	One who dances with beautiful steps in time with the music.
śaraṇagata jana varadē	One who gives boons to those who have taken refuge
kuvalayanayanē	One whose eyes are like the flowers of the water lily
kisalayacaraṇē	One whose feet are as soft as tender leaves
natajanapalana hṛdayē	Whose mind is ever engaged in protecting the humble
vikasita kamalasukō mala vadanē	One whose face is as beautiful and charming as a fully blossomed lotus
bhavabhaya samanē	One who destroys the fear of rebirth
vandē	I salute

ĀNANDA RŪPINIYE

ānanda rūpiṇiye tiraññu
amṛta svarūpiṇiye tiraññu
ajñāna nāśini jñāna pravāhini
ātma svarūpiṇi ennaṛiññu

I searched for YOu, the Immortal "One". I searched for You, the Blissful "One". You who are the destroyer of ignorance, the source of knowledge, I knew that You are the Divine Self.

kaṇṭuṟannīṭuvōr kandīla nin rūpam
kātōrttirunnavar kēṭṭīla nin nādam
kaṇṇaṭachīṭu kātaṭakīṭu
uḷḷil teḷiyum hṛdaya nivāsini

Those with their eyes opened could not see Your divine form. Those who were trying to listen keenly did not hear Your voice. Close Your eyes, close Your ears, She who resides in the heart will shine in Your own inner being.

ellā bhāgyaṅgaḷum maṟaññāl mātram
kiṭṭunna saubhāgyammē
ellā saundaryavum maṟannāl mātram
kiṭṭunna saundaryamē

You are the real fortune which is obtained when all fortunes are discarded, the beauty one beholds when all other attractions are forgotten.

uḷkkaṇ tuṟakkuvān śakti ēkīṭaṇē
unmattan ākkīṭanē
uḷḷil teḷiyunna nāḷ varēyum
kaṇṇunīril kuḷichīṭum ñān

Bestow on me the strength for the inner eye to be opened; make me intoxicated with divine bliss. Till the day You shine forth in my heart, I will be bathing in tears, I will be bathing in tears.

ĀNANDA SĀGARA

ānanda sāgara muralidharā
mīra prabhu rādhē śyām vēṇu gōpālā
nanda yaśōdā ānanda kiṣōrā
jai jai gōkula bāla jai vēṇu gōpāla

O Ocean of Bliss, Bearer of the flute, Mira Bai's Lord Radhakrishna, the Cowherd Boy who plays the flute, Son of Yashoda, the bliss of Kishora, victory to that Cowherd Boy of Gokula, the Flute Player!

ANANTAMĀYI PAṬARUNNA

anantamāyi paṭarunnōrākāśamē
antarangam āveśamāyuṇarunnu
ammē ambikē nityakanyē
nityē nirāmayē nirmalamē

The sky which is vastly expanding, vibrant with enthusiasm, the inner being, awakens. O Mother, Goddess Ambika, Eternal Virgin, the Eternal, the Blissful, the Immaculate.

arutarutē aviṭunniniyum
aṭiyane mōhitanākkarutē
anudinam viṭarumī hṛdaya vēdanakaḷ
aṟiññiṭumō nī hṛdayēśvarī

Never, Oh,.never again allow this suppliant to succumb to temptation. The pains of my heart are growing with the passing days; aren't You aware of it, O Goddess of my heart?

ammayillē enikkammayillē
paṟayū paṟayū ānandamē
ānandam vēndā ārōrum vēndā
nirmala prēma bhakti tarū

Don't I have a Mother? Is there no Mother for me? Tell me, O Blissful One, tell me. I seek neither bliss nor anything else; give me only pure love and devotion.

ANANTA SṚṢṬI VĀHINI

ananta sṛṣṭi vāhini
ananta bhāva śālini
anantate natēśvari
mahēśwari namō namā

Salutations to Thee, O Great Divine Goddess, Who art the Supporter of the entire creation, with infinite states and ever in the state of Supreme Dance.

amṛtānanda rūpiṇi
adharma rātri bhañjini
sudharma śarmapōṣini
prabhāmayi namō namā

Salutations to Thee, O Ever-Effulgent One Who art the Mother of Immortal Bliss, ever breaking the silence of the dead of night. Thou art the Protector of righteousness and wholesomeness in the world.

guru svarūpiṇi śivē
virāga mārga dāyini
mṛdu smitābha śōbhitāsya
pankajē namō namā

Salutations to Thee Who art in the form of the Guru. Thou art Goddess Shiva, showing the path of dispassion with a smile like a lotus flower.

manōmayi manōnmanī
jaganmayi sudhāmayī
satāmgati satāmmatī
sadā śivē namō namā

Prostrations to Thee, O Goddess Sadashiva the Consort of Shiva, Who art ever-present within the mind yet beyond the mind, Who art full of ambrosial bliss, Who guides through the true path, and Who gives the equanimity to follow that path.

svargamukti dāyinī
nisarga sarga kārani
cirantanī kirītini
prakāśinī namō namā

Prostrations to Thee, O Mother, who bestowest heaven and liberation. Thou art the Cause for everything in and beyond nature. Thou art beyond time, wearing the crown and effulgent.

prēma varṣini mahāgha
nāśini suhāsinī
mūla mantra rūpiṇi
sarasvati namō namā

Prostrations to Thee, O Saraswati, Who art ever showering divine love and Who destroys great sins and Who art the form of the Primal Mantra.

śrīkari cidambarī
śivaṅkari kṛpākarī
layankari mahēśi
bhadra kālikē namō namā

Prostrations to Thee, O Bhadrakali, the fierce form of Devi, Who art the cause for auspiciousness, permeating through the whole of consciousness, Thou art full of compassion and the cause for the submergence of individuality.

carācharātmikē samasta
viśvakārini namō
śivātmikē kalātmikē
bhavātmikē namō namā

Prostrations to Thee Who art present in all Creation and the Cause for the entire Universe. Thou art the life of Shiva as well as the life of the arts. Thou art ever-pure and absolute.

nirmalē nirākulē
nirankusē nirañjanē
nirgunē gunāśrayē
nirāmayē namō namā

Prostrations to Thee Who art ever pure, ever unruffled and Who art undifferentiated. Thou art the Absolute and the form of wholesomeness and the Abode of all qualities.

trikōnagē trilōcanē
triśūlini kapālinī
bhavāni bhāgya dāyinī
śmaśāna vāsini namō namā

Prostrations to Thee Whose form is like a triangle referring to the triangles in the Sri Chakra. Thou art the One with three eyes, Who carries the trident and wears a garland of skulls. O Bhairavi, Thou bestowest good fortune and live in cremation grounds.

akhaṇḍa jyōti caṇḍikē
alanghya śakti śaṅkarī
samasta yōga mārga
sampradāyikē namō namā

Prostrations to Thee Who art the Goddess Chandika full of radiance. Thou art Shankari, with Infinite Power. Thou art the Giver of all yogas and immortality.

caṇḍa muṇḍa khaṇḍana
pracaṇḍa ghaṇḍikāravē
niśumbha śumbha ghātinī
bhayankari namō namā

Prostrations to the One Who destroyed the evil demons, Chanda and Munda. Thou also destroyed Nishumbha and Shumbha. Thou art the Fierce One to evil-doers.

jhaṇal jhaṇal praghōṣa
khadgacālinī mahābalē
pravardhita prabhāva raudra
caṇḍikē namō namā

Prostrations to Thee Who swings Her Sword, making the sound "Jhana Jhana" and Who has infinite strength. Thou art the ever-increasing, effulgent and fierce Chandika.

brahmarūpa śaktirūpa
sarvarūpa dhāriṇi
parātparē parēśvarī
mahēśvari namō namā

Salutations to Thee Who art the form of Brahma, Shakti, the Essence of everything. Thou art ever beyond the Supreme. Thou art the Supreme Goddess.

satya dharma śanti prēma
mūlya samvidhāyikē
nitya śuddha buddha mukta
maṇḍale namō namā

Salutations to Thee who art the Bestower of Truth, Righteousness, Peace, and Love. Thy form is the eternal circle of Purity, Wisdom and Freedom.

AÑJANA ŚRĪDHARA

añjana śrīdhara cārumūrte kṛṣṇā
añjalī kūppī vaṇangīdunnen
kṛṣṇa harē jayā kṛṣṇa harē jayā
kṛṣṇa harē jayā kaithozhunnen

O Sridhara, Thou who art collyrium-hued and full of beauty, I salute Thee with joined palms. Victory to Krishna, salutations to Him!

ānandalaṅkārā vāsudēvā kṛṣṇā
ātaṅkamellām akattīṭanē

O Thou who art as beautiful as an ornament, O Son of Vasudeva, remove all my sorrows.

indiranāthā jagannivāsā kṛṣṇā
innende munbil viḷangīṭenē

O Beloved of Lakshmi (Indira), Master of the Universe, please shine before me.

irēzhulakinūm ēka nāthā kṛṣṇā
izheñchu dikkum vanangīdunen

O Krishna, Supreme Lord of all the fourteen worlds, I bow to Thee with joined palms.

unnigopālakā kamala netrā kṛṣṇā
uḷḷatil vannu vilangīṭēṇē

O Cowherd Boy, lotus-eyed Krishna, come and shine in my heart!

ūzhiyiḷ vannu pīṛanna bālā kṛṣṇā
ūnam kūṭāttenne pālikkane

O Krishna, Who art born as a Divine Child on earth, protect me in every way.

ennuḷḷil uḷḷoru tapam [klēśam] ellām kṛṣṇā
ennuṇṇī kṛṣṇā śamippikkane

Please destroy the grief in my heart, O darling Krishna.

eṭalar bananu tulya mūrtē kṛṣṇā
eṛiya mōdenā kaitozhunnēn

O Krishna with a body equal in beauty to Cupid, with great joy I salute Thee with joined palms.

ayihikamāya sukhattinkal āgraham
alpavum tōnalle gōpabālā

O Cowherd Boy, let me not feel even the least bit of desire for worldly pleasures.

oṭṭallā kautukam antarange kṛṣṇā
ōmal tirūmenī bhangi kānān

O Krishna, I am full of the desire to see the beauty of Thy dear, auspicious Form.

otakuzhal viḷi meḷamōde kṛṣṇā
ōṭi varikende gōpabālā

O Cowherd Boy, please come running, playing Thy flute!

saundarya kōmala keliśīlā kṛṣṇā
saubhāgya sampattu sāmathi tāye

O generous, beautiful and playful Krishna, please grant me good fortune, wealth and prosperity!

ambātiyiḷ paṇḍu veṇṇayu pāl param
āshayāl bhakṣicha vāsudēvā

O Vasudeva who long ago ate butter, milk and fruit in Ambadi.

APĀRA KRIPĀLŌ

apāra kripālō arikil nī vāyō
avanīśvarā kṛṣṇā aruḷvaram tāyō
arimullappuñciri akatāril viriyikkū
azhalpō ennātmāvu kuḷiraṇiyān kṛṣṇa

O boundless Compassionate One, come beside me. O Lord of the Earth, Krishna, confer upon me my desired boon. Let Your jasmine bud-like smile blossom in my heart, cooling it and making all sorrows disappear.

kanivinte tikavuttorazhakarnna nayanattin
oḷiyālennakatā ronnuzhiyān nī vā
kanal kattum hṛdayāntarāḷattilittiri
karuna mazha coriyān nī akatāril vā kṛṣṇa

With Your beautiful eyes, full of boundless compassion, shed light on my inner being. Come like a compassionate rain in the inner recess of my heart which is burning like a hot ember, Krishna.

maṇi murali kayūti naṭamāṭi vā mama
manamandirattil nī niṛaññāṭi vā
śrutilaya sangīta rasadhārayatilūten
matilaya sukhalābha gatinalku nī
kṛṣṇā matilaya sukhalābha gatinalku nī

Come dancing while playing Your sweet flute. Come dancing and fill the temple of my heart. Playing the music which is perfect in pitch and feeling, Krishna, give me the gift of experiencing the mind dissolve into You. Krishna, give me the pleasure of my mind's dissolution.

APĀRA SACHIT

apāra sachit sukha
sāgarame amṛtānandamayī
agati janattinnabhayam nīyē amṛtānandamayī
mātā amṛtānandamayī

Amritanandamayi, Shoreless Ocean of Existence, Consciousness and Bliss. Thou art the refuge for destitutes, O Mother.

azhal veyilēttu taḷarna
manassi nuṇarvintamṛtāṇ ammā
kara kāṇāttoru kaṭalallō nin karuṇāmṛtarasa
hṛdayam

Mother, Thou art the elixir of energy for minds weary of the hot sun of sorrow. Thy heart is a shoreless sea of ambrosial compassion.

kanivozhukum tava mizhimunayālen
karalinnaka monnuzhiyū
anavaratam tava caraṇasmaraṇayil
muzhuki uṇarṇṇozhukīṭān

Kindly touch the inner recess of my heart with a merciful look through the corner of Thine eyes so that I may be awakened forever and immersed in the incessantly flowing remembrance of Thy Feet.

snēham kondu manuṣya manasukaḷ
tazhukum dharayuṭe mātē
sadayam nī kaikkoḷḷuka yennuṭe
hṛdayam pūjāmalarāl

Mother of Earth, who caresses the bosoms of people with love, kindly accept this offering of my heart as the flower of worship.

ĀRAṚIUNNU

āraṛi unnu nin mahā vaibhavam
māyā prapaṇcattinādhāramē
āyiram āyiram ā jīva rāsikal
tēṭunnorādivya tējasmitam

Who indeed knows Your grand scheme? You are the very basis of this phenomenal world. All the millions of living beings search for You alone, search for Your Divine Luminosity.

jīvita bhāvamāyi jīvente jīvanāyi
jīva kāruṇya pratīka māyi
snēhātirēka svarūpamāyi mevunna
jīvāmṛta nandinī - dēvī
jīvāmṛta nandini

O Goddess, You are the very essence of life itself, the dispenser of compassionate intervention in the movement of life, and Your very nature is that Love that sustains all.

tāpasārādhini tāpa samhārini
tāpasānugraha bhāva nāngi
tāruṇyamē mana
lāvanyame varū
tāraka sopānamē dēvī
tāraka sopānamē

You are the One worshipped by the afflicted, the Remover of their afflictions, Whose pose is that of the Bestower of blessings on all. You are the very ladder that takes us to the dizzying heights of the stars.

ARIVĀYI AMṚTĀYI

aṟivāyi amṛtāyi akamalaril ciram
amarunnakhila carācara jananī
azhakin niṟavē - aṟivin tikavē
amṛtānandamayī bhava śamanē

O Mother Amritanandamayi, You are the Mother of all, of both the moving and unmoving, who dwells in the inner lotus as Supreme Knowledge and Divine Nectar. You are the fullest expression of beauty and knowledge, O Mother, who brings the cycle of transmigration to its end.

uṣassāyi uṇarvāyi ulaka poruḷāyi
maruvum sura muni sēvita caraṇē
karuṇārṇavamē praṇavāmṛtamē
sakalāmaya duritāpaha nayanē

O Ocean of Compassion, the embodiment of the Pranava (the AUM sound), who obliterates all misfortunes by a mere glance, You are the new dawn, the new awakening, the fundamental Reality, whose Feet are worshipped by sages and gods.

śrutiyāyi layamāyi teḷinīr kuḷirāyi
sirakaḷil unarvāyozhukum taṭinī
karaḷin oḷiyē kavitāmṛtamē
kadana smṛtikaḷe māikkuka jananī

O Mother, You are the stream of vitality that flows through my veins. You are the melody and the harmony of music, You are the coolness of pure fresh water. O Light of my heart, the inspiration of my poetry, please erase all memories of sorrow that I harbour in my mind.

kanivāyi tuṇayāyi anavaratam hṛdi
tanalaruḷum sura taru vallari nī
pularittēn malar kānti katiroḷi
vitaṛum bhuvana manōhara vadanē

Aren't You really like the celestial wish-fulfilling tree that gives shade within the heart, with Your never-ending kindness and readiness to come to my aid? O Mother, the whole world finds the radiance emanating in all directions from Your face, resembling the honey-filled flower at dawn, supremely exhilarating.

ĀSA NAŚIKKĀTTORĀ

āsa naśikkāttorātura manassē
ālōlamāṭum manassē
āzhamezhum azhaḷāzhiyil āzholā
ātmāvil ārati uzhiyū manassē
ātmāvil ārati uzhiyū

O mind, you are a busy harbour of desires, constantly buffeted by their flow. Beware, don't drown in the deep ocean of sorrow. Instead, do arati to the Atman — keep your attention focused on the Self.

ālambamillāte āndhyattil āpatich-
ākulamākum manassē
ātaṅka muktikkāyi, ānanda labdhikkāyi

ātmāvil ārati uzhiyū manassē
ātmāvil ārati uzhiyū

Beware, if you keep up like this, in the end you will fall without any real support, and be full of remorse. If you cherish Eternal Bliss, if you covet Liberation, then meditate, O mind, meditate on your Source.

ārṣa gāthāmṛtam ādarichācami
chāśā nirāśatthilūṭe
āsura bhāvam pōyi ātmāmṛtābdhiyil
āmajjanam ceyka nī manassē
āmajjanam ceyka nī

Meditate on the Ocean of Bliss within, give up your demoniac qualities, and follow the teachings of the Divine chants.

ĀTMA RĀMA ANANTA NĀMA

ātma rāma ananta nāma
ānanda mōhana śrī parandhāma
māyabhirāma mānasa prēma
sundara nāma suguṇabhirāma

ātma rāma	Delighter in the Self
ananta nāma	Of infinite names
ānanda mōhana	Blissful Enchanter
śrī parandhama	Supreme Goal
māyabhirāma	Charming
mānasa prēma	Having a mind full of love
sundara nāma	Having beautiful names
suguṇabhirāma	Charming, excellent qualities

AYŌDHYA VĀSI RĀM

ayōdhya vāsi rām rām rām
dasaratha nandana rām rām rām
patita pāvana jānaki jīvana
sītā mōhana rām rām rām

ayōdhya vāsi ram	Rama who stays in Ayodhya
dasaratha nandana	Son of Dasaratha
patīta pāvana	Purifier of the fallen
jānaki jīvana	Life of Janaki (Sita)
sīta mōhana	Enchanter of Sita

BĀLAKṚṢṆAKAM KALAYA

bālakṛṣṇam kalaya sakhī sundaram
kṛṣṇam kalaya sakhī sundaram
anganāmanganām
antarēmādhavō
mādhavam mādhavam
cantare nānganā
itthamakalpite
mandale madhyakam
sanchitau vēṇunā
dēvakī nandanam
śrī kṛṣṇa gōvinda harē murārē
hē nātha nārāyaṇa vāsudēva

Oh my friends, the beautiful and youthful Krishna is calling. O my friends, the beautiful and youthful Krishna is calling. O ladies, hand in hand, worship Krishna. Let us all go to Krishna. There is one Krishna between each of us and the Lord is in the middle of the dance circle as well. With the captivating music of His flute, He is inviting you to come. Devaki's Son (Krishna) is inviting you to come.

BHAGAVĀNĒ BHAGAVĀNĒ

bhagavānē bhagavānē
bhaktavatsalā bhagavānē

O Lord, O Lord, Who art loving towards devotees, O Lord.

pāvana pūruṣā pāpa vināśana
pāpikaḷ mātramāyi pāridattil

O Immaculate Self, Destroyer of sins, only sinners are left on this Earth now.

nērāya mārgaṅgaḷ nalkuvān ārundu
nārāyaṇā nanma pōyī maṛaññū

O Narayana, who will show the right path, for the virtuous have all vanished?

satyadharmādikaḷ naṣṭamāyi marttyaril
tatvaṅgalēṭil mātram otungi nilppū

Mankind has lost truth and righteousness and spiritual principles are confined only to books.

kāṇunnatokkeyum kāpaṭya vēṣaṅgaḷ
katiṭū kaṇṇā dharmam vīndeṭukkū

Everywhere only masked faces are seen. O Kanna, please protect and reinstate righteousness.

BHAJA GOPĀLA BHAJA GOPĀLA

bhaja gopāla bhaja gopāla
pyārē murārē mērē nanda lālā
nandalālā nandalālā nandalālā yadu nandalālā (2x)

bāla gōpāla bāla gōpāla
murali manōhara nandalālā
nandalālā nandalālā nandalālā yadu nandalālā (2x)
kōyī rāma bōlē kōyī śyāma bōlē
kōyī bōlē rādhe śyām
kōyī bōlē sītārām

Sing the names of Gopala, the Destroyer of the demon Mura, my dear Son of Nanda. Baby Krishna, Flute Player, Enchanter of the mind, Son of Nanda. Some call Him Rama, some call Him Shyama.

BHAJA GŌVINDA GŌVINDA

bhaja gōvinda gōvinda gōpāla
bhaja murali manōhara nandalālā

Pray to Govinda (Krishna), Lord of the cows, the Cowherd Boy, Pray to Nanda's darling, Enchanter of the mind, Who plays the flute.

BHAJAMANA MĀ

bhajamana mā mā mā mā
bhajamana mā mā mā mā
ānandamāyi mā mā

ānanda rūpa mā mā
bhajamana

Worship the Mother, The blissful Mother, The Mother Whose Form is Bliss

BHAJŌ MANA RĀMAKṚṢṆA

Bhajō mana rāmakṛṣṇa jaya bōlō
raghukula bhūshana rāma rāma rām
rādha mādhava śyāma śyāma śyām
harē rām harē rām
harē kṛṣṇa harē rām
harē kṛṣṇa harē rām
rām rām harē harē

O mind, pray to Ramakrishna. Say, "Victory to Him!" You are the Ornament of Raghu's race, O Rama. You are the Enchanter of Radha, O Krishna. O Lord Rama, Lord Rama, Lord Krishna, Lord Rama. O Lord Krishna, Lord Rama, Rama, Rama, Lord Hari, Lord Hari.

BHAVA MŌCAKA BHAYA

bhava mōcaka bhaya bhañjaka paramēśvara śaraṇam
mati nāyaka mṛti nāśaka tripurāntaka śaranam

O Supreme Lord Shiva, Bestower of Salvation, Remover of fear, Guide of my intellect, Destroyer of death and of Tripura[1], please give me refuge.

[1] Tripura, literally "the three cities", symbolically represents attachment to the three bodies, i.e. gross, subtle and causal.

sakalēśvara sarvōttama pari pāvana mūrtē
satatam tava caraṇāmbujam abhayam śubha mūrtē

O Lord of All, most splendid of all, supremely pure Being, let me take refuge forever at Your Lotus Feet, O Auspicious One!

śaśi śēkhāra śama dāyaka sura sēvita bhagavan
kalayāmyaham aniśam tava manamōhana rūpam

O Lord with the crescent moon on His crown, Bestower of forbearance, worshipped by all the gods, I meditate unceasingly on Your enchanting form.

śiva śaṇkara hara śaṇkara bhava śaṅkara śaraṇam
hara śaṅkara śiva śaṅkara śaraṇam tava caraṇam

O Bestower of auspiciousness, I take refuge at Your feet.

BHAVĀNI JAI JAI

bhavāni jai jai bhavāni jai jai
kailāśa śakti śiva śaṅkari jai jai
namah śivāya ōm namah śivāya ōm
namah śivāya ōm namah śivāy - ōm
bhavāni jai jai

Victory, victory to the Consort of Bhava (Shiva), Mt. Kailasa Shiva's Energy. Victory to the Giver of Auspiciousness. Salutations to the Auspicious One!

BHŌLANĀTHĀ RĒ

bhōlanāthā rē kāśīnāthā rē
dīnanāth hē thu viśvanāth hē thu

parvatīnāthā bhōlanāthā rē

O Lord of the innocent, O Lord of Kashi City, You are the Lord of the weak, and the Lord of the Universe.

ādināthā rē ānandadātā rē
kailāśa nāthā rē jñānapradātā rē
narttana sundara damaru kā nāthā rē
rakṣā karō mērē śāntīpradātā rē

You are the Primordial Lord and the Bestower of bliss. O Lord of Mount Kailas, Bestower of Knowledge, O Graceful Dancer, holding the damaru drum, please save me, oh Bestower of peace.

triśūladhārī rē trinētradhāri rē
maṅgalakārī rē samsāraharī rē
gangādhārī rē jagadōpakārī rē
darśan dō mērē jagadōdhārī rē

O Wielder of the trident, You Who have three eyes, Bestower of auspiciousness, Destroyer of the cycle of birth and death, Holder of the Ganges River, O Benefactor of the Universe, appear before me, O Redeemer of the world.

CENTHAḶIR PĀDAṄGAL

centhaḷir pādaṅgaḷ
cintichu cintichu
antarangattile cinta nīṅgī
santāpa muktanāyi
santatam vāzhuvān
nin snēha tīrttham pozhikukammē

Pondering over the lilac-bloom of Thy feet, all other thoughts have vanished from the mind. To remain ever free from sorrow, Mother, please pour out the Holy Waters of Thy Love.

anti chuvappinṭe cantam ūṟunna nin
mandahāsattin madhuvozhukkī
en karaḷ tāpam keṭuttiyen jīvane
nin kazhal tārōṭaṇachiṭāmō

By showering on me the honey of Thy smile, beautiful like the red hue of dusk, will Thou quench the fire in my heart and adhere my life to Thy Feet?

janma janmāntara puṇyaṅgaḷāl ninte
dhanya cintakken manam vazhangī
eṅkilum ententanartham sahippū ñān
nin kazhal tāriṇa kandu kūppān

By the virtues collected over many lives, there came in my mind the inclination towards divine thoughts of Thee. Yet, how many calamities do I face to have a glimpse of Thy Feet and offer my salutations!

CHŌḌ DE MANSĒ

chōḍ de mansē dukha kī cintā
nit yē sumir tū satya rē
dēh tū nahī man bhī tū nahī
tū he ātmā jān lē

Give up thoughts of sorrow and remember always that you are the Truth. You are neither the body nor the mind, know that you are the Atman (self).

hār gayā tū khōj mē sukh kē
is jaga kē saba bhōga mē
paramānanda he tērē antar
kabhī vahān tō jhāmk rē

In the attempt to find a lasting happiness through indulgence in material pleasures alone you have met with defeat. The undying happiness is within you, that is where it should be sought.

mē tum kē is bhēd mē manvā
nahī he śānti jān lē
ēk hī ātmā sab mē he tū
hī sab mē he vyāpt rē

Know that as long as you entertain the thought of "I" and "you" as separate entities then you will never know peace. The same consciousness is in all beings, the inner essence in you pervades all others.

ātmā sāmrāya kā tū he mālika
manvā tū kabhī dīna nahī
paramaśakti kā srōt bhī tū he
manvā tū kamsōr nahī

You are the master of the kingdom of the Self, you are never poor. Neiter are you weak; you are the source of supreme power.

CINTAKAḶKANTYAM

cintakaḷkantyam vannen antarangathil ponthum
santātānandattinte cantamām prakāśamē
pontaḷir pādaṅgaḷē cintichu cinthichivaḷ
santhōṣamāyitanne santyajichallō sarvam

O Glorious Light of Eternal Bliss, dawning within me when the thoughts have ended, pondering on Thy Golden Feet, I have happily given up everything.

svantamāyi nīyuḷḷappōḷ bandhukkaḷ vēnda vēre
svārthattintavidyayum satvaram dūrattākkū
cintiyennāśasūnam tāntamāvillī manam
kāntiyil layichēttam śāntiye bhujikkaṭṭe

When Thou art there as my own, I need not have any other relatives. Give up quickly the ignorance of selfishness! This mind will not be gloomy any more as it has shed the flower of desire. Let it dissolve in Luster and enjoy peace.

gandhavāhanan pōle bandhichu sarvattilum
bandhamillātte vāzhānuḷḷil nī vasikkaṇē
cintiykku manujā nī enthināy jīvikkunnū
janthuvargatte tanne pintuṭarunnō nīyum

Please dwell within me to help me live like the air, having contact with everything but having connection with none. Think, O man, why are you living? Are you living like an animal?

CUṬṬUNĪRI

cuṭṭunīri pukaññu kattunnoren
hṛttinittiri snēhāmṛtam tarū
bhakta dāsarkku dāsiyākunnoren
dukham ārō ṭuṇarttēndat ambikē

Please give just an iota of Thy ambrosial love for this smoldering, burning, inflamed heart. To whom else shall I, the servant of the servants of devotees, tell my woes, O Mother?

niṣkaḷaṅkamām bhakti lābhattinnāyi

etra nāḷāyi namikkunnu nin padam
bhaktavatsalē muktipradāyini
tṛkkaram toṭṭanugraham nalkanē

Since how long have I been bowing down to Thy Feet to gain devotion immaculate? Thou, Who art compassionate to devotees and Who art the Bestower of Liberation, please bless me with a touch of Thy hand.

svanta bandhu varānanē nīyozhi-
ññilla mattārumuttavarāyini
ninnilūnnunna nanya cetassukaḷ
pinneyum bata pāram tapikkayō

O Beautiful One, there is no one left other than Thee as my true friend and relative now. Tell me, do those minds which are totally and solely devoted to Thee have to suffer further?

entinenneyī andhakārattilē
kunti nīkki vaḷaykkunnu pinneyum
antharaṅgam kadanāzhi nīṅguvān
nin kṛpāmizhiyennil paṭikkaṅē

Why push me further into darkness? Won't Thou please glance at me with Thy compassionate eyes to remove the ocean of my sorrow?

pāññaṭukum mahāvipat sandhiyil
dēhi dēham vidum pakṣi kūṭupōl
nēṭi vechatum nēṭān sramichatum
kūṭe vannīṭukillatu nirṇayam

Like a bird leaving the cage, the soul will depart from the body at the moment of a great disaster which is fast approaching. Whatever one has gained or tried to gain will surely not follow him.

santatam manam samsāra sindhuvil
mungi māzhkunnu māyā mahēśvari
saṅkatakkaṭal vankara kēṛuvān
ambā nin pāda pōtam tarēṇamē

O Goddess of Illusion, the mind is ever sorrowful, being drowned in the ocean of mundane existence. Mother, please give me shelter at Thy Feet which is the boat to cross over this vast sea of misery.

DĀNAVA BHAÑJANA RĀMA

dānava bhañjana rāma rāma
śyāmala kōmala rām
hē rāma rāma jaya rāma rāma
rāma rāma rām
daśaratha nandana rāma rāma
daya sāgara rām
he dīnōm kē prabhu rāma rāma
rāma rāma rām

Rama, Destroyer of demons, dark-hued, soft and sweet Ram. O Rama, Rama, victory to Rama! Son of Dasaratha, Rama is an Ocean of Compassion. Those in misery are Your very own and You give delight to them.

DASARATHĀTMAJA

Dasarathātmaja dhanuja nāśana
rāmacandra dayānidhē
dēvakī sūtha dvārakādhipa
vāsudēva kṛpāmbudhe

I bow to You who are the Destroyer of demons, Dasaratha's son. O Rama, Crescent Jewel of the moon, kindness is Your wealth, O Lord of Dwaraka, Devaki's Son, the Ocean of Mercy, Vasudeva's Son.

sīta rām sīta rām sīta rām sīta rām
rādhē śyām rādhē śyām
rādhē śyām rādhē śyām
parama pāvana durita vāraṇa
rāmacandra namōstutē
patitarakṣaka bhava vināśaka
vāsudēva namōstutē
sīta rām

Extremely pure, Remover of difficulties, O Crescent jewel of the moon, Rama, I bow to You, O Vasudeva (Krishna), I bow to You.

raghu kulōttama ramaṇa vigraha
rākṣasāntaka pāhimām
yadukulōtbhava yatimanōlaya
sāndra sundara pāhimām
sīta rām

O Illustrious descendant of the Raghu dynasty, Your appearance is beautiful. O Destroyer of demons, protect me, O Ocean of Beauty.

bhuvana nāyaka punita mānasa
rāmacandra mahā prabhō
mṛti bhayāntaka kali malāpaha
vāsudēva namō namā

Lord of the earth, pure minded, O Crescent jewel of the moon, O great Lord Rama, I prostrate to You. I bow down to the Remover of the fear of death. I prostrate to Krishna Who obliterates the evils of the Kali age.

DAYA KARŌ HARI NĀRĀYAṆA

Daya karō hari nārāyaṇa
kṛpā karō hē jagat vandana
bhāvātita bhāgya vidhāta
dīna nātha anātha kē nātha

O Hari, Narayana, Lord of the universe, have mercy on me and shower Your Grace upon me. Beyond all conception, Lord of the helpless, You are the bestower of good fortune.

DAYĀ KARŌ MĀTĀ AMBĀ

dayā karō mātā ambā
kṛpā karō jananī
kṛpā karō mātā ambā
rakṣā karō jananī

kalyāna rūpiṇi kāli kapālini
karuṇā mayī ambā mām pāhī
ōm mātā ōm mātā
ōm mātā ānandamayī
ōm mātā ōm mātā
ōm mātā ānandamayī

O Mother, have mercy! O Mother, save us! Auspiciousness incarnate, merciful One, Mother Kali who wears a garland of human skulls[2], protect us. OM Mother, Embodiment of Bliss.

DĒVI DAYĀ KARI MĀ

dēvi dayā kari mā, amba
dēvi sarasvati mā
durga bhavāni mā, amba
kāli kapālini mā
jagadō dhāriṇi mā
amṛtānanda rūpiṇi mā

O Mother Goddess Giver of Compassion, O Mother Goddess of Knowledge, O Durga Consort of Shiva, O Mother Kali Consort of Kapali (Shiva), O Mother Support of the Universe, In the form of Amritanandamayi.

DĒVI DAYA KARŌ MĀ

dēvi daya karō mā
jai mātā gaurī kāli mā
dukha nivārō mayyā dēvi
bhakta janōmkē mayyā
maṅgala kāriṇi mā
jai mātā gauri kāli mā

mā, mātā, mayyā	mother
daya karō	be merciful
gauri	fair complexioned Devi

[2] representing the death of the ego

kali	dark complexioned Devi
dukha nivarō	remover of sorrow
bhakta janōmkē mayya	Mother of the devotees
maṅgala kariṇi	cause of auspiciousness

DĒVI MŪKĀMBIKĒ (AMMĒ AMṚTĒṢVARI)

dēvi mūkāmbikē[3] [ammē amṛtēṣvari]
oru varam tā oru nalvaram tā
dēvi mūkāmbikē [ammē amṛtēṣvari]
mānasa sauparṇikayūṭe tīrattil
maunamāyi vāzhum mūkāmbikē [amṛtambike]

O Devi, Silent Mother, give a boon, please give a benevolent boon, Thou who stays silently beside the Souparnika river of the mind.

rāgavum tālavum layavum nīye
kalayuṭe kaviyuṭe bhāvam nī
bhaktiyum nī muktiyum nī
mama hṛdayattin spandam nī

Thou art the tune, the rhythm, and the melody. Thou art the expressive Power of art and of the poet. Thou art Devotion and Liberation; Thou art the very beat of my heart.

vēdānta sāra sarvasvavum nī
ādimandhyānta vihīnavum nī

---

[3] Mookambika is a famous Devi temple n South India, by the side of the river Souparnika, in the state of Karnataka. The name means, "Silent Mother."

saguṇavum nī nirguṇavum nī
akhila [sakala] manasin ādhāram nī

Thou art the quintessence of Vedanta. Thou have neither beginning nor end. All forms are Thee and formlessness too. Thou art the substratum of all minds.

DĪNA DAYĀLŌ

dīna dayālō patita pāvani
kṛpā karō jananī
caraṇa kamal mē śaranāgata kō
abhaya dāna tuma dē dō (3x)

O Uplifter of the downtrodden, extremely compassionate Mother, grant me Your grace. Grant shelter to this refugee at Your lotus feet.

tērī karuṇā mṛdula pāvana sē
hṛdaya kamala khīla jāvē
manda manda muskān sē dil mē
candrika barasāve dēvi (2x)

Through Your compassionate and pure love the lotus of my heart will blossom. Your sweet, loving smile shines like the soothing beam of the full moon in my heart.

nayana nalīna sē karuṇā ras kē
saritā sadā bahāvō
amṛta dhāra mē
amṛta dhāra mē is anādha kō
amale tum naha lāvō (2x)

Through Your beautiful eyes, let the stream of compassion incessantly flow. In this flow of nectar, O Mother, bathe this lonely child of Yours.

jaga janani jaga pāvani mujh ko
jaldi tum apanāvo
viraha jalan ko
viraha jalan ko karunā jala se
buchāvo gōd me le lō (2x)

You who are the Creatrix and Sustainer of this Universe, use me as Your instrument soon. Extinguish the fire of separation with the water of compassion, and take me on Your lap.

DURGĀ AMBĀ BHAVĀNĪ

durgā ambā bhavānī jai jai
durgā ambā bhavānī
saṅkata hāriṇī maṅgala kāriṇī
praṇava svarūpiṇī mātā jai jai

durgā ambā	Mother Durga
bhavani jai jai	Hail to Lord Shiva's Consort
saṅkata hariṇi	Destroyer of sorrow
maṅgala kariṇi	Cause of auspiciousness
praṇava svarupiṇi	Of the nature of OM

DURGĀ NĀMAM

durgā nāmam uraiykkum pradeśam
etrayō pāvana puṇya pradeśam
dukhangaḷ okkeya kannu santōṣam
tatti kaḷikkunna divya sandēśam

The place where resounds the name of Durga, how holy and blessed it is! It is the divine message which removes sorrow and which fills one with mirth.

pāvani tan tiru nāmam japichāl
pātakamokkeyakannīṭumallō
sūrya prabhayil iruḷenna pōle
dūreyakalunnu śokaṅgalellām

If one chants the holy names of the Divine Mother, all one's sins will expire and sorrow will vanish like darkness before the sun.

bhūteśi ninṭe mahatvam aṟivān
bhūtala vāsikaḷ ajñarānammē
bhūri mōdāl nī kaṭākṣichu vennāl
bhūti paripūrṇa mākunnu sarvam

Goddess of all entities, we earthly beings are incapable of grasping Thy greatness. If Thou but cast a blissful glance, everything becomes auspicious.

dēvi mahēśī yōgeśī namastē
vaśyē viśudhē variṣṭhē namastē
vēda vēdyē vidyē nāthē namastē
ādi madhyānta vihīnē namastē

Devi, the Great Goddess, the Empress of Yoga, salutations! Salutations to the One of Whom the Vedas speak, the Wisdom, the Primordial Sound! Salutations to the One without beginning, middle, or end!

ĒHI MURĀRĒ

ēhi murārē kuñja vihārē
ēhi praṇata jana bandhō
hē mādhava madhu madana varēnyā
kēśavā karuṇā sindhō

O Destroyer of the demons Mura and Madhu, Kesava, Ocean of Compassion, Friend of all those who come to you with humility, Frequenter of the forest groves, O Blessed One having a lovely face, come to me.

rāsa nikuñje kuñjati niyatam
bhramara śatamkila kāntā kṛṣṇā
hē madhusūdana śāntā
tvām iha yācē darśana dānam
hē madhusūdana śāntā

O Krishna, serene Madhusudana, hundreds of honey-bees hover within those forest groves. Krishna, my frolicsome consort, I beg You for the gift of Your darshan, O serene Madhusudana.

nava nīrada dhara śyāmala sundara
candrika suma rucivēśa kṛṣṇā
gōpī jana hṛdayēśa gōvardhana dhara
vṛndāvana cara vamśīdhara paramēśa

nava nīrada dhara	One who steals butter.
śyāmala sundara	Darkly handsome one.
caruka	Charming.
sumaruci vēsa	Like flowers.
gōpi jana hṛdayēsa	Indweller of the Gopis hearts.
gōvardhanadhara	One who lifted the Govardhana mountain.
vṛndavana cara	One who roams about in Vrindavan.
vamśīdhara paramēsa	The Supreme Lord who carries a bamboo flute.

rādhā rañjana kamsa niṣūdana
praṇati stāvaka caraṇē kṛṣṇa
nikhila nirāmaya caraṇē

ēhi janārdhana pitāmbaradhara
kuñjē maṇdāra pāvane

O Enchanter of Radha, Slayer of Kamsa, Krishna, I prostrate at Your Feet, which remove all sorrow. O Janardana, clad in a yellow raiment, come to me in the Mandhara grove.

ELLĀ PULARIYUM

ellā pulariyum ente pratīkṣa tan
niṣpanda nimiṣangaḷ allō
ellā sandhyayum ente nirāśa tan
gadgada nimiṣangaḷ allō

O Mother, every sunrise seems like a succession of moments filled with all my expectations, and every sunset a series of instants replete with the welled up disappointments choking me inside.

uḷḷam eriññezhumī nedu vīrppukaḷ
kennu nin kālkal abhayam
unnidramāvunna tennā niniyente
kanmaṣa bhāra hṛdantam (2x)

When will these deep sighs, burning and rising up within me, find the refuge of Your Feet? When will this heart burdened with sin, be awakened?

karayunnu kaṇṇunīr illāte karaḷinte
uḷnāmbil poṭiyunnu bāṣpam
citaṛunnu cintakaḷ akalattu mizhinaṭṭu
maruvunnu tanayariṅgamme (2x)

I am crying, though no tears are shed; the cave of my heart is misty with teardrops. My thoughts are scattered everywhere. Mother, Your children stay back here with their eyes set on the horizon.

arutente tūlikakkī vyatha purṇamāyi
ālēkhanam ceytuṇarttān
patiyunnu kālkkalēk oru tuḷḷi kaṇṇunīr
atilunden ātma sandēśam

My pen is unable to find a way to express this anguish in words. Here falls a teardrop at Thy Feet which carries the message of my heart.

EṄGUPŌYI

eṅgupōyi ennōtoruvākku mindāte
kaṇṇan ārōmal kiṭāvu?
viṇṇu kaṟukkunnu kaikāl viṟāykkunnu
kaṇṇilīruḷ kanakkunnu

Where have You gone, Kanna, my darling baby, without saying a word? The sky is getting darker, my hands and legs are shivering, and darkness spreads over my eyes!

kāchiya paimbāl taṇukkunnu paikkulam
kaṇṇimaykkāte nilkkunnu
ponnin cilambocha ennorttu pōyaten
neñchin piṭappāyirunnu

The boiled milk is cooling down, the cowherds are watching with open eyes. I hear the sound of Your anklets, but alas, it is only my own heart beating.

uḷkkaḷam tiṅgi niṟaññu manassinte
kalpaṭavellām kaviññu

vatsalyabhāvam curannu nirannitā
pāl kaṭal pōle parannu

My mind is overflowing with emotions. Like the Ocean of Milk, affection is flowing without any limits.

cundile puñciri puntēnennōrttiṭṭu
vandukaḷ muttī muṟichō
kottī valichō kaniñña phalamennu
tettidharicha kiḷikaḷ?

Thinking it is honey, have the bees attacked You after seeing Your sweet, enchanting smile? Have birds come at You, thinking that You are an overripe fruit?

bhītiyāḷuḷḷil ippōzhum kuññukal
vēchu vēchallō naṭappu
kelppezhappūviḷam mēniyallē - mattu
kochuṇgaḷ nuḷḷi nōvichō?

I am frightened knowing that You can't even walk properly, being still a toddler. Have other youngsters been picking on Your tender body?

vēṇu gānattil kutirnolichippakal
vīṇa liññillāte pōke
ānāyapiḷḷēr maṟannō vāzhitetti
viṭettānuṇṇi valaññō?

Forgetting themselves as they listen to the flute, have they lost their way and made You wander around?

pāluṭṭukilla ñān kaṇṇane tāraṭṭu
pāṭiyuṟakkilla satyam
pūmēnī vāri puṇarilla kāṇkilum
kāṇātta bhāvam naṭikkum

I am upset and feel like not giving You any more milk. Neither will I sing You to sleep with lullabies or hug You. I will pretend that I haven't seen You even when I see You.

kai veṇṇa kākan kavarnennu poyi connu
kaṇṇaninnenne mayakki
kaṇḍattil veṇṇa kuruṅgumō kaṇṇante
kaḷḷattarangaḷāṇellām

He fooled me by saying that a crow has snatched the butter from Him. Will He get choked with butter? Anyway, these are only His pranks.

pinniludāññetti pinneyum kaṇṇanā
pālkkindi taṭṭi kamazhtti
pīli pareku kondānnu piṭaykkeyā
pāl kalam talli yuṭachu

Coming from behind, again Kannan has kicked the milk jug upside down. Beating with the tip of the peacock feather, He has broken the milk jug.

ellām maṛakkum ñān pinneyum kuññari
pallukaḷ kaṭṭicirikke
uḷḷam tuṭikkatirikkumō ammaykku
kallum aliññu pōvillē

I forget all His pranks when He laughs, showing His tiny teeth. Won't any Mother's heart beat heavily? Even a stone will melt.

EN MAHĀDĒVI LŌKEŚI

en mahādēvi lōkeśi bhairavi
enteyuḷḷam teḷikkāttatentu nī
cintanīyam amēyamen caṇḍikē

ninte līlakaḷ ōrōnnum atbhutam

Bhairavi, my Great Goddess, the Ruler of the world, why are Thou not enlightening my heart? O Chandika, imponderable, mysterious and wonderful are each of Thy plays.

ambē ninte kaṭākṣam tarēṇamē
ambayallātorāśrayam illallō
ambikē jagannāyikē bhūvil nī
kampamellām ozhikkaṇam cinmayī

Mother please look at me. There is no refuge other than Thee. Mother, the Ruler of the Universe, the Earth, the Essence embodied, please remove all my sorrows.

īśvarī nin savidhē vasikkuvān
sāśvathamāya mārgattilūṭenne
viśvamōhinī ennum nayikkaṇē
sacidānanda mūrtē tozhunnu ñān

O Goddess, Enchanter of the Worlds, please lead me through the eternal path so that I can abide near Thee forever. I bow to Thee the Embodiment of Consciousness, Existence and Bliss.

ninte kāruṇya meṅkalundākaṇē
tamburāti mahēśi mahēśvarī
ninte rūpamen cittattil ekiyen
antarātmāvil ānandamēkanē

Have mercy on me, O Maheshi, the Great Goddess. Please give joy to my inner self by providing Thy form to my mind.

EN MANA KŌVILIN

en mana kōvilin vātil turannu ñān
ammē ninakkoru pīṭhamiṭṭu

O Mother, I have opened the door of my inner sanctum, and prepared a ceremonial seat for You.

kaṇṇunīrālatu pērttum kazhu kīṭṭu
teṅgalāl pūmpaṭṭu ñān virichu

I have washed it totally clean with the stream of my tears, and spread a silken cloth on it with my sobs.

āsakaḷ kattichu dīpam koḷutti ñān
nāmaṅgaḷal niṛamāla cārtti

I have lighted a holy lamp, with my desires as fuel, and Your Name, unendingly repeated, became a sacred garland.

ellā guṇangaḷum certtu kattichu ñān
aṣṭa gandham puka cinnu tāyē

All of my personal qualities piled up and burnt have turned into the sweet smoke of frankincense.

ammaykku mātram orukkiya pīṭhattil
onnezhunaḷḷanē prēma mūrtē

Please enter and take that ceremonial seat specially prepared for You.

enneykku menne nin kālkkal arppicchu ñān
nin kāl chilambai māṛidaṭṭe

O, let me offer myself at Thy feet, and turn myself into Your chiming anklet forever!

ENNILE ENNE TIRIÑÑU

ennile enne tiriññu nōkkunnu hā
vismayam kāṇmatinnandhakāram
minnunnu ninnōrma aṅgiṅgithā hṛdi

allalla ñān innanātayallā

I am looking back at myself and wonder at the sight of darkness today. Thy memories are scintillating here and there within the heart. No, no more am I an orphan today.

poya kālam svapna tulyamāyi pōyinnu
jīvitam ninnil samārpippu ñān
entānini ceyitiṭēndatennamma nī
kandaṟiññenne nayikkēṇamē

Bygone days seem like a dream today. I am surrendering this life to Thee, Mother. Thou Thyself can only see what is best for me and lead me to perform the right actions.

nin snēha tūveṇnil āvoḷi tūki nī
en manappū viṭarttēṇamammē
māyāndhakāram keṭuttiyen mānasa
śrīkōvilil nī teḷiyukammē

By shedding the moonshine of Thy love, Mother, please let the flower of my mind blossom. Destroy the darkness of illusion, Mother, and shine forth in the temple of my mind.

ENTINĀṆAMME

entiṇānamme hara vakṣassiṅkal
padamūnnikondu nilppū nī
entāvām nī nuṇaññatennammē
nāvu nīṭṭikkāṇikkān

O Mother, why are You standing with both feet firm on Hara's chest? What did You taste that makes You stick Your tongue out?

eṭṭum poṭṭum tiriyāppeṇmaṇi
pōlallō nī naṭappatum
itutān nin pativennatambikē
aṟiyunnu ñānakatāril

You behave like a crazy girl. I know this is Your real nature also, O Ambika. Did Your Mother also stand on Your father's chest? Ambika, please tell me the truth quickly today.

bhīkaramenkilum ninmukham entoru
śōbhanam snēhamayam
nin maṭittaṭṭil kiṭannuṟangītuvā-
neṟunnu mōhamammē

Even though Your face appears fierce, still it is very bright and overflowing with love. My desire to sleep on Your lap is ever-increasing.

madyam kuṭicchu nī madicchu naṭakkunnu
vennu chollvū janaṅgaḷ
nitya satyamē nī nukarunnatu
amṛtāṇennāraṟiyunnū

People say that You drink alcoholic beverages to get intoxicated. But, O Immortal Truth, nobody realizes that what You are tasting is ambrosia. the divine nectar.

satvaguṇattāl ninnuṭe
cevaṭiyettīṭumenna tattvam
kāṭṭunnu tātante māṟil caviṭṭi nī
ēkuka sadguṇam mē

Cultivating divine qualities, one can reach Your adorable feet. This truth is revealed by Your standing on the Divine Father. Please grant me divine qualities.

ENTU CEYVŌ YEDU CEYVŌ

entu ceyvō yedu ceyvō
ente nandananē kandatillē

Alas! What to do and how? The Son of Nanda is not to be seen anywhere.

kālamē yezhunnēttavan kāṭṭil
kālikaḷe mēykkān pōyō

Or, getting up early in the morning, did He go to the forest to graze the cows?

paitaṅgaḷumāyi piṭichu
piñcu pādam oṭiññō daivamē

Or, O God, did He break His legs fighting with the other children?

mandi mandi cennīṭṭavan valla
kundilum māṛiññu vīṇō

Or, running here and there, did He fall into a ditch?

ETRA NĀḶĀYI AṬĪYAṄGAḶ

etra nāḷāyi aṭīyaṅgaḷ ī vidham
attalārnūzhalunnū dayānidhē
satya mūrte bhagavan kaniññīṭaṇam
bhaktavalsalā kṛṣṇā harē jaya

O Embodiment of mercy, we have struggled in this misery for so long. O Truthful One, have mercy on us. Victory to You, Krishna, the Friend of devotees!

entinālō narakattil ī vidham
unti eṭṭu valaykkunnu ñangaḷē
kuntidēvi tan putrare pottiyā
nin tiruvatī kṛṣṇā harē jayā

Why do you push us into this hell and torture us in this way? Victory to You, Krishna, the exalted One Who protected the sons of Kunti!

nityavum bhaval pādam namiykkumī
ente yācana kēḷkkumaṛākaṇam
ennuḷḷil bhakti ēṛumaṛākaṇam
jagannāyakā kṛṣṇā harē jayā

Krishna, be kind enough to listen to the entreaties of this one who bows down at Your Feet daily. Let devotion grow inside me. Victory to You, Krishna, Master of the Universe!

mannilāke niraññaruḷīdunnā
mannā kāruṇya mākum ciṛakatīl
enne nityam aṇacchu koḷḷēṇamē
jagannāyaka kṛṣṇā harē jayā

Take me under the wings of Your infinite Presence that fills the entire world. O Master of the World, Krishna, victory to You!

endinenneyī māyāyam sindhuvil
iṭṭu vaṭṭam kaṛakkunnitīvidham
tōnnanam kṛpā ezhayām ennil nī
bhagavāne kṛṣṇā harē jayā

Why are You tossing me about in the Ocean of Illusion in this way? Have mercy on this poor one. Protect me Krishna, victory to You!

pāpa bhārāluzhaññītum ennuṭe
pāpa bhārā maṛuttu dayāmayī
kāttu pālichu tuṣtiyēkēṇamē
pāpa nāśanā kṛṣṇā harē jayā

O compassionate One, protect and bring happiness to em who is struggling under the great load of sins, O Destroyer of sins. O Krishna, victory to You!

GANGĀJATĀ DHARA

(jaya) gangājatā dhara gauri śaṇkara
girijā mana ramana
śiva mṛtyuñjaya mahādēva maheśvara
mangala subhacaraṇā
nandi vāhana nāga bhūṣanā
nirupama guna sadhanā
natana manōhara
nīlakanta hara nīraja dala nāyanā
ōm hara hara hara mahadeva,
śiva śiva śiva śadāśiva
ōm namō namō namah śivaya

jaya gangajata dhara	Victory to the Who holds Ganga in His matted hair
gauri saṅkara	Gauri's auspicious Lord
girija mana ramana	One Who delights the mind of Her Who is born of a mountain (Parvati)
śiva mṛtyuñjaya	Auspicious Conqueror of death
mahādēva mahēśvara	Great God and Lord
maṅgala subhacaraṇa	Bestower of good fortune
nandi vahana	Whose mount is the bull Nandi
nagabhaṣana	Having serpents as ornaments

nirupama guṇa sa-dhana	Who is the source of incomparable Divine attributes
natana	Divine Dancer
manōhara	Enchanter of the mind
nilakanta	Bluethroated
hara	The Destroyer
niraja dala nayana	Lotus petallike eyes

GANGĒ SVĀRGANGĒ

gangē svārgangē gangē
pavitra bhāgīrathī
jaitra sañcārinī
bhāśura māyi pāvana māyi
pāpa nāśa jala vāhini gangē

Oh Ganga, oh heavenly Ganga, Thou art the pure Bhagirathi, the ever-flowing one. Thou art effulgent and purifying. Thou art the river whose water destroys all sin, O Ganga!

civa purātana sura vāhinī
tavasu pāvana jala dhārayil
manasu mantra japam ceytozhuki
uṣassu pōluṇaraṭṭe jīvitam ātma viśuddhi
vannunaraṭṭe jīvitam

Thou art most ancient and historic, the river of the gods. In thy spiritually purifying water, ever-flowing with the chant of mantras,

tunga himācala taṭini gangē
calita kutūhala caritē
hima dhavaḷīta maya gātrē gangē
dhruta gati jalati tarangē

O Gange, thou art flowing fast and having huge waves, emerging from the tall Himalayas with a snow-white body endowed with a moving and enchanting history.

manalaya kāriṇi
śubha nadi gangē
kaḷa kaḷa nāda tarangē
bhārata puṇya payasvini mātē
śama dama dāyini vandē
gangē gangē gangē

O Gange, thou causest the mind to merge. Thou art a pure river making the sound "kala kala." O blessed and enchanting Mother of India, Thou art the giver of control of the mind and senses. Prostrations to thee.

GHANA ŚYĀMA VARṆANTE

ghana śyāma varṇante vanamāli kannante
kāloccha kēlkkān kotichu
kaḷaveṇu nādattin lahariyiḷāṛādan
manamāke kōrittarichu

I had a great desire to hear the cloud-colored, garland-decorated Kannan's approaching steps. My mind was getting intoxicated at the thought of listening to His flute and getting immersed in it.

kandatillā sakhī karmukil varṇane
karunatan kaṭalāmen kaṇṇane
vanavalli kūṭilil maṛaññuvō kaṇṇan
ghanavēṇi rādhaye tēṭi

But I have not seen Him, the cloud-colored, ever-compassionate Kannan. Did He disappear in the flower bushes looking for the lovely-haired Radha?

rādhikē priya sakhi rādhikē
nī yetra bhāgyavati puṇyavati
munimārum nukarata sukha cakravāḷattil
puṇarunna pariśudhi nī rādhe
puṇarunna pariśudhi nī

O Radha, dear friend Radha, how lucky You are, how divine! Even the sages have not tasted as much purity as You. You are the love-incarnate whom even the gods are looking for.

yamuna yiliḷam tennal
svararāga sudhatûki
mama manam rāga samudramāyi
oru nēramenneyum kāṇātalayumō
yadu nandanā rādhā priyanē

When the enchanting breeze from the Yamuna River touched me, my mind became an ocean of love. Will Kannan ever wander, looking for me also?

GIRIDHARA BĀLA

giridhara bāla hē nandalālā
dēvaki nandana śyāma gōpāla
giridhara bāla hē nandalālā
rādhā mādhava rāsa vilōlā
bansi dhara hē śyāma gōpāla

giridhara bāla	The Boy Who held the Mountain
hē nandalala	O Son of Nanda
dēvaki nandana	Son of Devaki

śyama gōpala	Dark colored cowherd boy
rādha	Krishna's beloved
mādhava	Beloved of Lakshmi
rasa vilōla	Who played in the Rasa Dance
bansidhara	Who holds the flute

GŌPĀLA GŌVINDĀ GOVINDA

gōpāla gōvindā gōvinda harē murārī
mayura mukuta pitāmbharadhāri vṛndāvana
sañchārī jaya vṛndāvana sañchārī
gōpala gōvinda gōvinda harē murārī

O Protector of cows (Gopala) , O Krishna, You are the Lord of the cows, Slayer of the demon Mura. You walk around Vrindavan wearing the peacock crown, clad in yellow silk. Victory to You, who walks around Vrindavan. O Protector of cows (Gopala) , O Krishna, You are the Lord of the cows, Slayer of the demon Mura.

śaṅka cakra gada padmā dhāri
kṛṣṇa mukunda murārī
harē kṛṣṇa mukunda murāri

You hold the conch, the discus, the mace and a lotus, O Krishna, Bestower of Liberation, Slayer of the demon Mura, O Hari, O Krishna, O Mukunda, O Slayer of the demon Mura.

GŌPIYĒ CINTICHU

gōpiyē cintichu cintichu ñān oru
gōpikayākān kotichū
rādhikē ninne ninachū ninachū ñān
nin niṛamākān kotichū ammē

Contemplating the Gopis for so long, I also want to be a Gopi. Mother Radha, thinking constantly of You, I wish to attain Your complexion.

nin prēmam mādhuri alpam nukarnnu ñān
unmatta nākān kotichū
nin mahā bhāvatil alpam nukarnnu ñān
kaṇṇanil ākan kotichū ammē
rādhē rādhē rādhē rādhē

Drinking a little of Your sweet love, I want to be ecstatic. Mother, tasting a little of Your Great Divine Mood of Krishna, I want to merge with Krishna.

ā rāsalīlakaḷ ōrttōrttu ñān ahō
kāḷindi tannalayāyottu
ā muralīravam ōrttōrttu ñanahō
vṛndāvaniyai taḷirtu ammē
rādhē rādhē rādhē rādhē

Recalling the "rasa leelas" (divine play of Krishna and the Gopis on the banks of the Yamuna River), I become like a wave of the Kalindi (Yamuna) River. Mother, remembering these songs of the flute, I become the blooming garden of Vrindavan.

premendu paurṇami tūvoḷi tûkumen
mānasa tīrattilettū
rādhā priyaṅkara śyāmā manōhara
kaṇṇīr puzhayil tuṭiykkū vannen
rādhē rādhē rādhē rādhē

Come to the shores of my mind where shines the full moon of love. O beloved of Radha, oh blue complexioned one, swim in the full river of my tears.

GŌVINDĀ GŌKULA ĀYŌ

gōvinda gōkula āyō (2x)

Govinda has come to Gokul!

Īs gōkul usa mathura nagarī
bich bahat hē jamuna gahari
gōkul mē sukh mathura mē
dukh kamsa kō mukh kum lāyō jī āyō

In between the cities Gokul and Mathura flows the Jamuna river, there is happiness in Gokul and sorrow in Mathura. Kamsa, the evil one who will be destroyed by Krishna, has come.

nanda bhavana mē naubat bājē
ānand mē pyāri gōpiya nāchē
gōkul mē sukh mathura mē
dukh mangal mōda basayō jī āyō

In Nanda's palace there is a grand celebration and all of the Gopis dance in bliss. There is happiness in Gokul but sorrow in Mathura. Now auspiciousness and happines has come.

nanda kē ānanda bhajō jai kanaya lāl kī
hathī dīna ghōda dēna aur dīna pālki

Praise to Krishna, the joy of Nanda. Give eelphants, orses and palanquins to Krishna.

GŌVINDĀ GŌPĀLĀ

gōvindā gōpālā
bhajamana kṛṣṇa harē (2x)
he prabhū dīna dayāla
bhajamana śrī harē

gōvinda	Lord of the cows
gōpala	Protector of the cows
bhajamana kṛṣṇa harē	O mind, chant "Krishna Hari"
hē prabhu	O Lord
dīna dayala	Kind to the afflicted
bhajamana śrī harē	O mind, chant "Sri Hari"

GŌVINDA JAI JAI

gōvinda jai jai gōpāla jai jai
radhā ramana hari
gōvinda jai jai

Victory, victory to the Lord of the cows (Krishna), victory, victory to Gopala, victory, victory to Radha's sweetheart, Krishna.

GŌVINDA MĀDHAVA GŌPĀLA

gōvinda mādhava
gōpāla kēśava
jaya nanda mukunda
nanda govinda rādhē gōpāla
giridhāri giridhāri
jaya rādhē gōpāla
ghana śyāma śyāma śyāma rādhē
rādhe gopāla
jaya nanda mukunda nanda gōvinda rādhē gōpala

gōvinda	Lord of the cows
madhava	Beloved of Lakshmi
gōpala	Cowherd
mukunda	Bestower of Liberation
kēsava	Controller of the senses

nanda	Son of Nanda
giridhari	Who held the hill on His hand
ghana śyāma	Who is dark hued
rādhē	Krishna's beloved

GŌVINDA RĀDHĒ

gōvinda rādhē gōvinda rādhe
gōvinda govinda gōpāla rādhe
vēṇu vilōla hṛdaya gōpāla
gōvinda gōvinda gōpāla rādhē
bhakta vatsala bhāgavata priya
gōvinda gōvinda gōpāla rādhē

gōvinda	Lord of the cows
rādhē	Beloved of Krishna
gōpala	Cowherd boy
vēṇu vilōla hṛdaya	Flute player in the heart
bhakta vatsala	Lover of His devotees
bhagavata priya	Dear to the devotees

GURU CARAṆAM

guru caraṇam guru caraṇam
śrī guru caraṇam
bhava haraṇam
paramaguru caraṇam
bhava haraṇam
satguru caraṇam
bhava haraṇam
śiva guru caraṇam
bhava haraṇam

The Guru's Feet destroy the cycle of birth and death. The Supreme Guru's Feet destroy becoming. The Satguru's Feet destroy that cycle. The Guru's Feet, who is equal to Siva, destroy the cycle.

GURU MAHARĀNI

guru maharāni guru maharāni amṛtānandamayī
amṛtānandamayī mātā amṛtānandamayī
ōm mātā śrī mātā amṛtānandamayī
aṛabi kaṭal tīrattay amarum divya yōgini
amṛtānanda mayī dēvi
sāṣṭāṅgam praṇamichiṭam

I prostrate before Mata Amritanandamayi, the Queen of Gurus, the Divine Yogini, residing on the shores of the Arabian Sea.

ātma vidya nēṭānum
satdharmācaraṅattinum
bhukti mukti pradē dēvī
sāṣṭāṅgam praṇamichiṭām

I prostrate before the Goddess who grants both 'bhukti' and 'mukti' (worldly enjoyments and spiritual salvation), with the supplication that I gain in spiritual knowledge, and will be able to uphold 'dharma' (righteousness).

kāma kāṇcana lōbhādi
kāḷa kūṭa viṣaṅgaḷē
katti karichu viṭṭīṭum
kāḷi sātru vināśini

O Mother, You are verily Kali, the Destroyer of obstacles on the spiritual path, including the two deadly poisons of lust and greed.

bandhu villātto rēzhaykku
bandhuvāyi vilasēṇamē
bandha mōkṣaṅgal nalkunna
bandhuvē nitya kanyakē

To one (like me) who is without any kinsmen, O Eternal Virgin who bestows both bondage and Liberation, please be my next of kin.

śrī mātā śri maharājñī
śrīmat simhāsanēśvarī

Supreme Ruler of the Universe! Empress of the Universe!

GURU VĀYÛR PURA

guru vāyûr pura śrī hari kṛṣṇa nārāyaṇa gōpāl
mukunda mādhava muralidhāri nārāyaṇa gōpāl
mādhava madhusūdana hari nārāyaṇa gōpāl
mana mōhana muralidhāri murāri nārāyaṇa gōpāl
gōvardana giridhāri murāri nārāyaṇa gōpāl

guru vayûr pura	The One Who lives in Guruvayur
śrī hari	Vishnu
nārāyaṇa	Vishnu
gōpal	Cowherd
mukunda	Bestower of Liberation
mādhava	Beloved of Lakshmi
murali dhāri	Who holds a flute in His hand
madhusûdana	Destroyer of the demon Madhu
mana mōhana	Enchanter of the mind

gōvardana giridhari Who held the Govardhana Hill aloft

HARI HARI ŚRĪ HARI

hari hari śrī hari śaraṇam śaraṇam
hari śrī hari hari śaraṇam śaraṇam
śaraṇam hari hari śrī hari śaraṇam
hari caraṇāmbujam aniśam śaraṇam

O Lord Vishnu, give us refuge! Lord Hari's Lotus Feet are always our refuge!

uraga śayanan ulakapālakan
praṇava payōdadhi valayita nilayan
vyāpana śīlan viṣṇu pradhānan
kēvala caitanya kēdārabhūtan

Salutation to Lord Vishnu, Who sleeps on the serpent Ananta, Protector of the world, Whose abode is surrounded by the sacred ocean of milk, Whose nature is all-pervading, Who is the Embodiment of Absolute Spirit.

niyama rūpan nikhilādhāran
sakala samsāra duritāpahāran
anubhava sāra rasāmṛta rūpan
nikhila nigamānta sārātma rūpan

He is the Guiding Figure and Support of all, Who removes all worldly sorrows, Who is the Essence of the nectar of Divine Experience, the Quintessence of the Upanishads.

HARI ŌM

hari ōm hari ōm hari ōm hari ōm
hari hari hari ōm

mujhe lāghi lagan hari darśan kī
hari darśan kī

I am longing for the vision of the Lord

jaise ban me papihā man me
papihā man me
āśa kare nitha darśan kī
hari darśan kī

Just as the papiha bird sings only one note, my mind longs only for the vision of God.

gale vana mālā mukuta viśālā
mukuta viśālā
pītha vasan sundar thanu kī
hari darśan kī

You are beautiful wearing a garland of wild flowers and a majestic crown and yellow cloth.

man katti ūpar caraṇ na nūpar
caraṇ na nūpar
kar mē gadā sudarshan kī
hari darśan kī

The Lord has auspicious marks and anklets on His feet. He is holding a mace and the Sudarshan Chakra (discus) in His hands.

brahmānandā pyāsu manu māhi
pyāsu manu māhi
caranu kamala yuga paraṣanu kī
hari darśan kī

Brahmananda (name of the ancient author) has this longing in his mind, to merge in the Lotus Feet of the Lord.

HĒ BHAVĀNI HĒ DAYĀNI

hē bhavāni hē dayāni hē mahēṣi namō namō
śaṅkari dēvi namō namō
śakti brahmāni namō namō

O Consort of Lord Shiva (Bhava), Merciful One, Great Goddess, salutations, salutations. O Divine Energy, Consort of Lord Brahma, salutations, salutations.

HĒ GŌVINDA HĒ GŌPĀLA

hē gōvinda hē gōpāla hē dayālanā
prāṇa nātha anātha sakhē
dīna durita nivār

hē samartth agamya purān
mōha māyā kār

hē	Oh
gōvinda	Lord of the cows
gōpala	Protector of the cows
dayālanā	Merciful One
praṇa nātha	Lord of life
anātha sakhē	Friend of the orphans
dīna durita nivār	Remover of the misfortunes of the helpless
samartth	Omnipotent
agamya	Unknowable
puran	Ancient
mōha maya kar	Cause of the illusion of attachment

andhakup mahā bhayānak
nānak pāl udhār

Nanak prays, "O Merciful One, remove me from this fearful dark well.

hē mādhavā
hē mādhavā madhusūdhanā
dayā karō hē yadu nandanā
hē yādavā muralidharā
śyāma gōpālā giridhara bālā
nanda nandanā govindā
navanīta cōrā gōvindā
mathurā nāthā gōvindā
murali manōhara gōvindā
gōvindā govindā rādhē śyāma gōvindā
nandakumārā gōvindā
navanīta cōrā gōvindā

hē mādhava	O Consort of Lakshmi
madhusûdhana	Slayer of the demon Madhu
daya karō	Be merciful
hē yadu nandanā	O Son of the Yadu dynasty
hē yadava	O one belonging to the clan of Yadavas)
muralidhara	Holder of the flute
śyāma gōpala	Dark colored protector of the cows
giridhara bala	Child who held aloft the mountain
gōvind a	Lord of the cows
navanita cōra	Stealer of butter
mathura nātha	Lord of Mathura city
murali manōhara	Who enchants the mind by the flute
nandakumara	Son of Nanda

HĒ NĀTH AB TU

hē nāth ab tu aisī dayā hō
jīvan nira taku jāne napāye

O Lord, at least now, be kind enough to see that fighting the battles in life, I do not become tired.

yah man na jāne kyā kya karāye
kuch ban na pāyā apane banāye

When will this mind propel me to do actions according to its whims and fancies? I do not know. I have not succeeded in becoming anything by my own making.

samsār me hī āsakta rahakar
din rāt apane matalabhu kī kaha kar
sukha keliye dukh lākhōm śaran par
ye din abhi tak yō hī bitāye

Remaining attached in this world, doing actions according to my selfish desires, experiencing sorrow trying to gain happiness, I have passed all these days this way,

aisā jagādō phir sō nā jāvūm
apane kō niṣkām prēmi banāvū
mem āp kō chā hū ōr pāvu
samsār kā me rahe kuch na jāye

Wake me up in such a way that I do not fall asleep again. May I desire and obtain You alone. Let not the fears of the world remain even a bit.

baha yōgyatā dō sat karma karlūm
apne hṛdayame sat bhāvu bharlūm
naruttan hē sādhan

bhava sindhu karlūm
aisā samayi phīr āyena āye

Make me fit to always act righteously; may goodwill fill my mind. Let me cross this ocean of transmigration. Who knows if such valuable moments may come again or not?

hē nāth mujje nirbhimāni banādō
dāridra haralō dāni banādō
ānanda me bhī jñānī banādō
mē hum tumhāri āśā lagāye

O Lord, make me humble, removing all false pride. Remove poverty and make me charitable. Make me blissful, make me a Realized Soul. I remain always longing for You.

HĒ RĀM HĒ RĀM

hē rām hē rām
jag mē sucō tērā nām
tū hī mātā tū hī pitā hai
tū hī tō hī rādhā kā śyām

O Rama, Rama, Your name pervades the whole world. You are the mother, You are the father, and You are indeed Radha's Krishna.

tū antaryāmi sab kā svāmī
tērē caraṇōm me chār dām
tū hī bigāde tū hī savāre
is jag kē sāre kām

You are the Indweller of all created beings. You are the Lord of everything. Your feet are the abode of all. You are the day and the night. Worshipping You should be the only activity in the world of all created beings.

tū hī jagadhāthā viśva vidhāthā
tū hī subah tū hī śyām
tū hī gītā tū hī rāmāyan
tū hī tō hē vēdpurān

You are the Creator of this Earth and all beings in it. You control the whole universe. You are morning, You are evening. You are Bhagavad Gita, You are Ramayana, You are the Essence of all the Vedas and Puranas.

HṚDAYĀÑJALĪ PUṢPA

hṛdayāñjalī puṣpa kalitāñjalī amba
kavitāñjalī sāma gānāñjalī
madhurāñjalī bhāva
bharitāñjalī amba
puḷakāñjalī bāṣpa mukuḷāñjalī

Mother, adoration of the heart, adoration with plucked flowers, adoration with poetry, adoration with Vedic songs, adoration sweet, adoration full of passion, adoration with hairs standing on end, adoration with the flower buds of tears.

amṛitēśvarī amba śaraṇam sadā hṛdī
viḷayāṭaṇē pada malarēkanē
janakōṭikal kōṭi stutigītikal
pāṭī pukazhttīṭunnu manam kuḷirtīṭunnū

O Mother Amritesvari, You are my refuge forever. Please sport in my heart and let me hold on to Your flowery feet. Millions of people sing Your glory with a multitude of songs in praise, hearing which, the mind is refreshed.

matimōhanam dēvī karuṇāmṛtamṛta

kathakaḷ dayāmayī mahadāścaryam
karaḷ nont "ammē" ennu karayumpōzhe - makkaḷ
karatār koṭuttamma karayēttunnū

Devi, the Merciful, Your ambrosial stories of nectarous Grace enchant the intellect and are wonderful. The very moment Your children cry out "O Mother" with heartfelt pain, You extend Your flowery hands and pull them to the shore.

amṛtēśvarī amba bhuvaneśvarī
kāmya varadāyinī prēma sura vāhinī
karuṇāmayī kaṇṇinima pōlamme - kāttū
kaniyēname nanma coriyēṇamē

Mother Amritesvari, Goddess of the Universe, Bestower of desired boons, Who holds the wine of Love, O merciful one. As eye-lids protect the eyes, kindly protect us and shower on us all good fortune.

HṚDAYĒŚVARĪ EN HṚDAYA

hṛdayēśvarī en hṛdaya vipañchiyil
uṇarunna svara rāgam nī

O Goddess of my heart, You are the musical note and the 'raga' that rises up on the lute that is my heart.

ā nāda lahariyil ñān ennum darśikkum
vidyā sarasvati nī – en jīvita sarvasvam nī

I will always see Your form, O Sarasvati, Goddess of Learning, in the intoxication of that sound. You are my all in all.

nin mṛdu hāsamen anta rangattilor
āyiram ventiṅgaḷāyi
nin kaṭākṣattinte kāruṇya tennalil
ñān aliññillāteyāyi

Your gentle smile has turned into a thousand crescent moons in the deep inner recesses of my mind. My personal identity has been carried away by the gentle breeze of Your compassionate glance.

nin cālanaṅgalinnōrōnnumennuṭe
sundara svapnaṅgaḷāyi

Every single one of Your actions have turned into sweet dreams for me.

nin tiru nāmam innenne piriyātta
cintā malaru kalāyi

Your holy name always stays with me, always blossoming in my thoughts.

nin cāru rūpaminn ōmanichīṭāttōr
ōrmakaḷ illāteyāyi

There are no memories left in my mind which do not contain Your lovely form.

en hṛdayēśvari ende hṛit spandanam
nin kīrttanālāpamāyi

O Deity of my heart, my very heartbeats have become songs of devotion to You.

INDIRĒ SUBHA MANDIRĒ

indirē śubha mandirē
ghanasāra candana carchitē
sundarī sura vandinī
jana vṛnda vandya padāmbujē

O Indira, the upholder of auspiciousness, O beautiful one adored by the gods, You are worshipped by multitudes of people with devotion.

ennil vannuḷavāyitunnora-
nartha jāla mozhicchu nī
mandahāsa samētamennuṭe
mānasē vilasēṇamē

Please remove all the troubles on my path. Please remain with me with a smiling face.

sūrya kōṭi samānanē
taruṇārkka candra vilōcanē
pāvanī sukha dāyinī
śubha sāmagāna vinōdinī

Your face is as bright as ten million suns. Your eyes are like the rising sun and moon. You are so pure. You destroy the illusory world.

bhēda mokkeyozhichu durgati
nīkkiyakkare pūkuvān
yōgyamāyor anugraham taru-
īśvarī jagadīśvarī [amṛtēṣvari]

To get over sadness and ill fate and then to cross Maya, please grant me Your blessings, O Mother of the Universe.

IṄGAKALE NINNE KĀṆĀN

iṅgakale ninne kāṇān uzharunnu
etrayō kātattin appuṛam nī
eṅgane ñān ammē nin cāru rūpatte
oru nōkku kandiṭum prēma mūrtē

I long to see You, O Mother, but You are so far away, miles and miles away. How can I have a glimpse of Your beautiful form, just a glimpse, from this far away?

entu pizhachu ñān enne tanichākki
itra vēgam vīndum pōyiduvān
vīndum enikki vidhiyeṅkil pāriṭa
jīvitam ennatin arthamentu

What wrong did I perpetrate? For this to be my fate, to be left alone while You are gone again, contemplating the meaning, if any, of this life.

āroṭu collum ñān en manō vēdana
ārundu nī yallā tīśvarī col
onnōṭi vanniṭu ninne ninachu ñān
orō nimiṣavum eṇṇi nilppū

With whom shall I share my agony? Who else is there for me? Tell me, O Goddess, and please come rushing back. I am counting each passing moment.

INNALLŌ KĀRTIKA NĀḶU

innallō kārtika nāḷu
ennamma piranna nālu
saundaryam viḷangum nāḷu
santōṣam pūkum nāḷu

Today is the Kartika star (Amma's birth star), that day when my Mother was born, that day when happiness and auspicousness permeate everywhere.

ñaṅgaḷe dhanyarākki
ñaṅgaḷe mattarākki

ñaṅgaḷe bhrāntarākki
ñaṅgaḷe śantarākki

We have become mad with joy, divinely intoxicated. We also feel grateful and are at peace with ourselves.

snēham pakarnnu nī āvōḷam tannu
ellām marannu ñānatu nukarnnu
nin divya snēhattin pakaram nalkuvān
ilammē en kayyil onnummilla

You fed me from the fountain head of love. I forgot myself and imbibed as much of it as I could. But alas, Mother, I have nothing to give You back in return, nothing at all that will match your divine love.

janmadina sammānamentu nalkumammē
enteyī janmam ñān ninnilarppikkām
enteyellām nī ñān ninte dāsan
satakōṭi vandanam karuṇāmayī

What can I give to You as birthday present, Mother? Let me dedicate my life to You. You are my everything, and I am Your servant. Oh Mother, the Embodiment of Compassion, millions of prostrations to You.

IRUḶ TIṄGI VAḶARUNNA

iruḷ tiṅgi vaḷarunna vanabhūmiyil
oru karal nontu karayunna karivandu ñān
poriyunna vayarinnu pāśi nīkkuvān – ammē
prabha tūku malar kandu madhu vundiṭān

O Mother, this honey-bee is starved because it is too dark in this dense forest to spot the honey-filled blossoms. Please shed some light — I am weeping my heart away.

jani tannu tikavutta manurūpavum - ammē
mati tannu tiru [hari] nāma mura ceytiṭān - ī
vidhi vanna vazhiyentu karaḷ nīṛuvān? itu
hitameṅkil ivannilla etir bhāvavum

O Mother, You gave a me human birth just so that I would chant the Lord's Name with all my heart. Why is it my destiny to cry in this agony? If this is Your desire, I have no word against it.

aṣṭikku vazhi tēdi paṭi yettuvān ammē
bhikṣaykkāyi ninavilla, nahi pātravum
kṣuttinnu perukunnu mama kukṣiyil tava
mṛdu bhakti lata tannil amṛtēkumō

O Mother, this one does not know how to get to Your doorstep to seek his daily sustenance. This one does not even have a begging bowl that is worthy of the food You give. But the hunger to sip honey from the sweet creeper of bhakti (devotion) is increasing each day.

sthala mundaṅgadhikam nin pada tāratil - tava
pada bhakta tanayarkku viḷayāduvān
sarvam nin pada tāril kaṇi kandiṭān oru
nōṭi nēra mivanamma iṭayēkaṇē

The space within Your mind is large enough to accommodate all of Your devotees. Please find a brief moment to help me surrender all at Your Feet.

JAGADHŌDHĀRIṆI MĀTĀ

jagadhōdhāriṇi mātā durga
jagadhōdhāriṇi mā
jāgō jāgō mā jāgō jāgō mā jāgō jāgō mā janani

jai gauri dēvi rana caṇḍi dēvi
hē śiva ramaṇī jāgō mā
jaya jagadhōdhārini mā

jagadhō dhāriṇi	Support of the world
mātā durga	Mother Durga
jagō mā	Awake, O Mother
janani	Mother
jai gauri dēvi	Hail to the Goddess Consort of Lord Shiva
rana caṇḍi dēvi	Goddess who is fierce on the battlefield
hē śiva ramaṇī	Who is pleasing to Lord Shiva

JAGADĪŚVARI JANAMANAHĀRINĪ

jagadīśvari janamanahāriṇī
paramēśvari paśupati ramaṇī
patitāvani pāvani jananī
mati dāyini māyini layinī

śivarañjini śāmbhavi śivadē
paśupāśa vimōcana mahitē
munimānasa śōbhini śubhadē
śaranāgata pālini sukhadē

ajavāsava vandita caraṇē
kamalōpama sundara nayanē
nigamāgama varṇita caritē
karuṇāmayi kāmita varadē

mṛduhāsa suśōbhita vadanē
paripāvana mōhana naṭanē
karuṇārasa sāgara hṛdayē
sakalāmaya hāriṇi kalayē

jagadīsvari	The Goddess of the Universe
janamanahariṇi	The capturer of the minds of people
paramēśvari	The supreme Goddess
pasupati ramaṇi	The giver of happiness to Lord Shiva
patitāvani	One who is adored by the afflicted
pāvani	The pure one
janani	Mother
matidāyini	The giver of intelligence
mayini	The great enchantress
layini	The great destroyer
śivarañjini	The one who is united with Shiva
śambhavi	Another name for Goddess Durga
śivadē	The giver of auspiciousness
paśupāśa vimōcina	The remover of the cords of attachment
mahitē	The great one munimanasa
munimanasa sōbhini	Who shines in the minds of saints
śubhadē	The deliverer of happiness
śaranāgatapālini	The protector of the refuge seeker
sukhadē	The giver of pleasure
ajavasavavandita caraṇē	Whose feet are worshipped by brahma and Indra
kamalōpama sundara nāyanē	The one whose eyes are so beautiful, like lotuses in full bloom

nigamagama varṇita caraṇē	Glorified by Nigamas and Agamas
karuṇamayi	Compassionate
kāmita varadē	Giver of desired boons
mṛduhasasu sōbhita vadanē	Whose face is beautified by a sweet smile
paripāvana mōhana naṭane	Pure and enchanting dancer
karuṇarasa sāgara hṛdaya	Whose heart is an ocean of compassion
sakalāmaya hāriṇi	The destroyer of all sorrows
kalayē	The great artist

JAI JAI JAI DURGĀ MAHARĀNI

jai jai jai durgā maharāṇi
jai jai jai durgā maharāṇi

Victory! Victory! Victory! O Durga, the Great Queen.

darśan dō durgā maharāṇi
darśan dō durgā maharāṇi

O Durga, the Great Queen, grant me Thy Vision.

viśva kō mōhit karne vāli
tīn lōk mē rahne vāli
jagbharni janani varadāyi
darśan dō durgā maharāṇi
darśan dō durgā maharāṇi

O Enchantress of the Universe, O Mother Who dwells in all the three worlds, Thou art the One Who gave birth to the whole creation and Thou art the Bestower of all boons. O Durga, the Great Queen, grant me Thy Vision.

pāp nāś karlene vāli
bhaya dukh sab harlene vāli
simha vāhini mā kalyāni
darśan dō durgā maharāṇi
darśan dō durgā maharāṇi

O Mother Durga, Thou art the One Who destroys all ignorance and Thou art the One Who removes all fears and sorrows. O Mother who is seated on a lion, Thou art the embodiment of all auspiciousness. O Durga, the Great Queen, grant me Thy Vision.

śraddhā karunā bhakti rūp tum
chāyā māyā śakti rūp tum
hṛdaya vāsini ambe bhavāni
darśan dō durgā maharāṇi
darśan dō durgā maharāṇi

O Mother, Thou art the very personification of faith, compassion, and love, and Thou alone art the Great Illusion, the Supreme Power. O Mother Bhavani, Thou dwell in all hearts. O Durga, the Great Queen, grant me Thy Vision. Victory! Victory! Victory! O Durga, the Great Queen!

JAI JAI KĀLI MĀ

jai jai kāli mā (6x)
jai jai bhaya bhañjini kāli mā
jai jai bhava tāriṇi kāli mā
jai jai jagadīśvari kāli mā
jai jai jagadkāriṇi kāli mā

Victory to Kali, who is the remover of fear, who takes You across Maya, who is the Mother and Cause of the Universe.

jai jai tripurasundari kāli mā
jai jai tribhuvanēśvari kāli mā
jai jai kṛpā sāgari kāli mā
jai jai śyāma sundari

Victory to Kali, who is the enchantress of Shiva, who is ever-compassionate and who is dark and beautiful.

jai jai mahāyōgini kāli mā
jai jai mahāmōhini kāli mā
jai jai bhakti dāyini kāli mā
jai jai mukti dāyini

Victory to Kali, who is the greatest yogini, who is the greatest enchantress, who bestows bhakti and mukti

jai jai mātru rūpiṇi kāli mā
jai jai prēma rūpiṇi kāli mā
jai jai brahma rūpiṇi kāli mā
jai jai śakti rūpiṇi

Victory to Kali, who is the Mother of all, who has love for all, who is in the form of the Formless and who is also Energy.

JAI MĀ JAI KĀLI MĀ

jai mā jai kāli mā mā jai kāli mā jaya mā
jaya kāli dēvi
jaya mā jaya kāli dēvi
jaya jaya mā jaya kāli dēvi

jai mā jai (durga, pārvati, lakṣmi, śārade)

Jai mā	Victory to Mother.
Jai kāli mā	Victory to Mother Kali
jaya kāli dēvi	Victory to Goddess Kali

JAI MĀTĀ DĪ MĒRĪ MĀ

jai mātā dī mērī mā
mērā man tērī vihār
bahut dukhi hē ye sansār
muche bachāvō mērī mā

Salutations to the Mother! O my dear Mother, my mind is Your residence. This world is full of sadness. Please save me, my dear Mother.

jai paramēśvari jai jagadīśvarī
jai bhuvanēśvarī rājarajēśvarī

Salutations to Paramesvari (wife of Lord Shiva), Salutations to Jagadisvari (the Lord of all the world), Salutations to Bhuvanesvari (the Lord of the earth), Salutations to Rajarajesvari (the Queen who rules over all the rulers).

mātā kāli śmaśānavāsini
mātā durga simhavāhini
mahishāsura kā anth kāran
muche bachāvō mēri mā

Mother Kali dwells in the cremation grounds; Mother Durga is seated on the lion. You who put an end to the life of the demon Mahisha, please save me, O my dear Mother.

madurai mīnākṣi kanyakumāri
kāñchi kamākṣi mā karumāri
gāttā hum mē gīt tumāri
muche bachāvō mērī mā

Goddess Minakshi of Madurai is a young girl; Goddess Kamakshi of Kanchipuram is Mother Karumari. I am singing Your glories; please save me, O my dear Mother.

JAI ŚĀRADĒ MĀ

jai śārade mā jai śārade mā
ajñānata se hamem pār de mā

O Mother Sarada (an aspect of Devi; Goddess of Knowledge), Take us across the shores of ignorance.

tū svar ki devi ho sangīt tuchhse
har sabd tera ho har gīt tuchhse
ham hai akele ham hai adhūre
teri śaran mem hamem pyār de mā

You are the Goddess of Sound; music comes from You. Each word is Yours, each song springs from You. We are lonely, we are fragmented, we seek refuge in You; give us Your Love.

muniyōm ne samachhī
guniyōm ne jānī
vedōm ki bhāshā purānōm kī vānī
ham he kyā samachhe
ham he kya jāne
vidyā ka ham kō adhikār de mā

The language of the Vedas and the words of the Puranas (epics) are understood by the sages and the virtuous ones. What can we grasp? What can we know? Give us the right to acquire knowledge, O Mother.

tū śvet varnī devōm ke devī
hāthōm me vīnā gale me sūmālā
manse hamāre mithā de andhera
ham kō ujālōm ka samsār de mā

You are white-complexioned, You are the Goddess of gods. You hold a veena in Your hands and wear a beautiful garland on Your neck. Destroy the darkness from our minds and give us the world of light.

JAI SARASVATĪ

jai sarasvatī
namō namō tava caraṇam
jai sarasvati
namō namō mama jananī

Victory to the Goddess of Knowledge, salutations to Your Feet, victory to the Goddess of Knowledge, O my Mother.

JAYA JAGAD JANANĪ

jaya jagad jananī jagadambē
mātā bhāvāni mātā ambē
jai jai jai jai jai jagadambē
jai jai jai jai jai mātā ambē
mātā ambē, mātā ambē, mātā ambē
mātā bhāvāni mātā ambē

Victory to the Universal Mother, to the Divine Mother of the universe, Siva's consort, Mother Divine. Victory, victory, victory, victory, victory to the Divine Universal Mother. Victory, victory, victory, victory, victory to Mother Divine. O Mother Divine, O Mother Divine, O Mother Divine, O Mother, Siva's consort, Mother Divine.

JAYA JAYA MAHEŚVARĪ

jaya jaya mahēśvarī bhakti mukti pradē
jagadudaya kāraṇē kāruṇya vāridhē
manataḷirilepozhum ninne stuticchiṭum
mama hṛdiyanāratam narttanam ceyyaṇam

O Maheswari, Bestower of devotion and liberation, Cause of the world, O ever-compassionate One, please dance in my heart constantly as I always praise You in my mind.

jani mṛiti nivāraṇam bhava taraṇa tārakam
madhu mathana sēvitam muni jana niṣevitam
hari hara viriñcādi lāḷitam tvalppadam
mama hṛdiyanāratam narttanam ceyyaṇam

You are the remover of death and birth. You take us across the ocean of transmigration. You are worshipped by Brahma, Vishnu, Shiva and all the sages and seers.

jaya jaya śivātmikē śakti svarūpiṇī
mahitaguṇa śālinī pañca bhūtātmikē
vibudhajana sēvitē viditabudha pūjitē
mama hṛdiyanāratam narttanam ceyyaṇam

You are the power behind Shiva. You are endowed with all divine qualities. You are the force behind all the five elements in nature. You are worshipped by all wise men. Please dance in my heart.

maṛajñāna poraḷāyi maṛayōrku vandyāyi
maṛakaḷkkumappuṛam nilkkum ambē
maṛanālum vazhttum manōharam tvalppadam
mama hṛdiyanāratam narttanam ceyyaṇam

You are the wisdom contained in all the Vedas. You are also beyond the Vedas and scriptures. You are highly qualified to be worshipped by Vedic scholars and seers. All four Vedas praise Your enchanting feet.

sakala duritāpaham kaivalya dāyakam
bhānu kōṭi prabham bhaktajanārchitam
kēvalānanda pradāyakam tvalppadam
mama hṛdiyanāratam narttanam ceyyaṇam

You are the remover of all bad luck. You bestow Liberation on the deserving. You shine like tens of millions of suns. Let Your feet, which are worshipped by devotees and which are the bestowers of pure bliss, dance in my heart always.

JAYA MĀ JAYA MĀ

jaya mā jaya mā
jagadīśvari pāhi mām
jagadīśvari sarvēvari
bhuvanēvari pāhi mām

Victory, victory to Mother. Protect me, O Empress of the Universe. O Empress of the Universe, Empress of all, Empress of the Earth, protect me.

JAYA ŚIVA ŚAṄKARA

jaya śiva śaṅkara jaya abhayaṅkara
sāmba sadāśiva
śiva harare śiva harare śiva harare
jaya śiva śaṅkara jaya abhayaṅkara
jaya gangādhara jaya bimbādhara
vyāgrāmbhara dhara

śiva harare śiva harare śiva harare

jaya siva saṅkara	Hail to the Auspicious One
abhayaṅkara	Giver of fearlessness
samba sadasiva	Ever auspicious
harare	The Destroyer
gangadhara	Who holds the Ganges river on His head
bimbadhara	Who wears the crescent moon
vyagrambharad-hara	Who wears a tiger skin

KALA MURALĪ

kala muralī ravalōla mukunda
kali vīṭākkuka karaḷ, gōvindā
kavi jana kalpana puṣpa vimānam
karalitu tāvaka ratna vimānam
nirupama sundara viśvakamānam
tava naṭanōtsava ranga vitānam

O Mukunda, enchanting flute player, please make my heart Your playhouse. My heart is the golden chariot in the poet's vision; it is Your chariot also. With Your presence it is the most beautiful mansion in the world.

oru piṭiyavalālanupama bhāgyam
oru tariyilayālamṛta nivēdyam!
tirumizhi nīril nanañña nicōlam
pakaruka draupadimārkkabhimānam

One handful of flattened rice was the turning point of happiness; one leaf became the offering divine. Save the honor of all the Draupadis in the world with the blessed offering of Your endlessly flowing shawl.

eḷiya vanennum kaṇṇā nin sakhi
eḷya mulantandanupama lahari
yadukula bālanu pīlittirumuṭi
yatikaḷil yati nī rāsavihāri!

You are always fond of the lowly and deprived, O Kanna. The worthless piece of bamboo (the flute) is a source of unequaled joy. The Boy from the Yadu dynasty has given such a high status even to a peacock feather. You are the greatest sage among all sages, O enchanting rasa dancer.

KĀLCHILAMBOCHA

kālchilambocha kēlkkāttatentē kaṇṇan
kāṇāmaṛayattu pōyi maṛaññō?
kanmaṣanāśanan kaṇṇanen cētassin
daṇḍam nivarttichiṭāttatentē?

Why can't I hear the tinkling of Kanna's anklets? Has Kanna gone away to a far away place? Though Kanna is the remover of all afflictions, why is He not removing the sorrow of my heart?

kaṇṇīr kaṇaṅgaḷām pūvukaḷ kaṇṇante
kālkkalarppikkān ñān kāttirippū!
tāmasam tellum varāte kaṇṇan mana
kkaṇṇil teḷiññullasichṭēṇam! kaṇṇā (6x)

I am waiting to offer my tears as flowers at His feet! May Kanna shine in my mind without any delay!

kāṇātirippatinentu ñāyam mana
kkaṇṇinte kāzhcakkuṛavinālō?
kāruṇya mūrttiyām kārmukil varṇṇante
nērmizhichāyi vennilūnniṭēṇam kaṇṇā(6x)

I wonder why I can't see Kanna. Is it because of the blindness of my mind's eye? May the eyes of the Embodiment of Compassion, the cloud complexioned One, be fixed on me!

centāmarākṣane cintichu vēṛuḷḷa
cintakaḷ tāne nilachupōṇam
prēmātmarūpattil āzhnen manam sadā
sāyujyasaukhyam nukarnnu pōṇam

Let all thoughts stop by thinking of the Holy eyed One! My mind, by immersing in that lovable form, should ever taste the bliss of union!

KĀLI DURGE NAMŌ NAMĀ

kāli durgē namō namā
kāli durgē namō namā
śakti kuṇḍalīnī namō namā
kāli durgē namō namā
ūmā pārvati namō namā
kāli durgē namō namā

Salutations to Kali and Durga, to the Kundalini Śakti, to Uma and Parvati (Daughter of the Mountain Himalaya)

KĀLI MAHĒŚVARI PĀRVATI

kāli mahēśvari pārvati śaṅkari
śaraṇam śaraṇam śaraṇam mā
śaraṇam śaraṇam śaraṇam mā

O Kali, Great Empress, Daughter of the Mountain (Himalaya), Auspicious One, I seek refuge again and again.

dukha vināśini durgā jaya jaya
kāla vināśini kāli jaya jaya
umā ramā brahmāni jaya jaya
rādhā rukmini sītā jaya jaya (2x)

O Durga, Destroyer of sorrow, O Kali, Destroyer of Time, O Parvati, Lakshmi and Sarasvati, O Radha, Rukmini (Krishna's Consort) and Sita, victory, victory!

KĀLINDI TĪRATTU

kāḷindi tīrattu ninnum
muralī gānam kēlkattatente?
kaṇṇanteyā vanamāla tūkitum
saugandha vātamiṅgettāttatentahō?

Why can't I hear the music of the flute from the banks of the river Kalini? Why is the sweet wind not blowing here, taking the aroma of Kanna's garland made of forest flowers?

kīṛippiḷarunnu neñcakam poṭṭunnu
nīrippukayunnu praṇaṅgaḷum sakhī!
ennātmanāthan manōharan mādhavan
ennarikattuminnumettāttatentahō?

Friend, my heart is tearing and breaking. My vital airs are fuming! Why is the Hero of my soul, the Handsome One, Madhavan, not coming near me today?

rāvēṛe chennuvō pātirāvāyatō?
ā śyāmacandran udichuvō malsakhī?
paurṇṇami rāvinnamāvāsiyāyitō?
sīta samīraṇan tīttirayāyitō?

My dear friend, has the night advanced so much? Is it passed midnight? Has that dark moon risen? Has the full moon night turned into new moon night? Has the cold wind turned into a heat wave?

nīla prakāśamāyi kūriruḷāyavan
ennātma vāniṭam mūṭikkaḷaññuvō?
pēmāri peyyunna santāpa mēghamāyi
jyōtirmayan śyāmanāyaten karmamō?

That Blue Effulgence has become, as it were, pitch darkness. Thus, has He covered my mind's sky. Is it my fate that the Glorious One, who has become a sorrowful cloud which rains down heavily, has turned into the Dark One?

KAṆṆĀ KARIMUKIL VARṆṆĀ

kaṇṇā karimukil varṇṇā, ālila
kaṇṇā nṛttamāṭū
ente manassile vṛndāvanattin
nikuñjattil nṛttamāṭu
kaṇṇā nṛttamāṭu

O Kanna, with the complexion of the rain clouds, Who rests on the leaf of the peepal tree, dance, O dance in the Vrindavan of my mind.

nandakumārā navanīta cōra
nannāyi nṛttamāṭū
tittōm tām kiṭa kiṭatōm tām
kiṭa kiṭatōm tām tittaiyyam nṛttamāṭu
manattozhuki parakkunnitātirā
tārangaḷ tan prabhāpūram
ōṭi varu kaṇṇā māṭi viḷikkunnu

ennile yamunā tīram
bālagōpāla vṛndāvana lōlā
ālolam nṛttamāṭu
tittōm tām kiṭa kiṭatōm tām
kiṭa kiṭatōm tām tittaiyyam nṛttamāṭu

O Son of Nanda, Stealer of fresh butter, dance elegantly. Dance to the rhythm of the music. The radiance of the stars is spreading all over the sky, O Child Gopala. The bank of the river Yamuna within me is inviting Thee to dance, dance vigorously. Dance to the tune of the music.

kāṭum meṭum tōzharum uṇaraṭṭe
pāduka vēṇugōpāla
kāṇatte ñaṅgaḷ mati varuvōḷavum
rādhā mādhava līla
nitya nirāmaya
nirupama sundara
nirttāte nṛttamāṭu
tittōm tām kiṭa kiṭatōm tām
kiṭa kiṭatōm tām tittaiyyam nṛttamāṭu

O Gopala, sing. Let the forest, the valleys and the friends awaken. May we see the play of Radha and Madhava to our hearts content. O Ever Wholesome One, the Incomparably Beautiful One, dance without break. Dance to the tune of the music.

KANNANDE PUNYA NĀMA

kaṇṇande puṇya nāma varṇaṅgaḷ
karṇṇattilennu kēḷkkum ñān?
karṇṇattil kēṭṭu kōlmayir kondu
kaṇṇīrilennu muṅgum ñān?

kaṇṇīril muṅgi śudhanāyi nāmam
tannattānnennu pāṭum ñān?
tannatān pāti mōdattāl maṇṇum
viṇṇum ennu maṛakkum ñān?

maṇṇum viṇṇum maṛannu bhakti sam
pūrṇanāyennu tuḷḷum ñān?
tuḷḷikkaḷichen samsāra kaḷa
kaḷḷikaḷennu māykkum ñān?

akkaḷam māykkum kēli tuḷḷaliḷ
aṭṭahāsam ennārkkum ñān?
aṭṭahāsattāl śudhi dikkukaḷ
keṭṭinumennu nalkum ñān?

āṭṭavum kazhiññammatan maṭi
taṭṭilēykkennu vīzhum ñān?
vīṇumammatan śītaḷānkattil
sānandam ennuṛaṅgum ñān?

uṛaṅgumbōzhuḷḷil karimukil varṇṇan
tiruvuṭalennu kāṇum ñān?
uṇṇarumbōl munnil kāyāmbū varṇṇam
kandu kandennuṇarum ñān?

When will I hear the auspicious names of Kanna in my ears? On hearing, when will I horripilate and become immersed in tears? Immersed in tears, I will become pure, and in that state of absolute purity, when will I sing the names spontaneously? When am I going to forget the earth and the sky in the ecstasy of singing spontaneously? By forgetting the earth and the sky, when am I going to dance with full devotion? Upon dancing, when am I going to rub off the soiled marks on the world stage? In that playful dance, which will enable me to rub them off, I will cry out loudly. When will I be able to give purity to the eight directions by my loud cry? When will I finally fall into my Mother's lap after the play has been enacted? On falling on my Mother's lap, when will I sleep soundly? When will I be able to see the beautiful form of Lord Krishna in my heart during my sleep? On waking up, when will I wake up seeing the world enchanting form of Lord Krishna?

KAṆṆANIṄGETTUMŌ TŌZHI

kaṇṇaniṅgettumō tōzhi tōzha
rādhayōṭottu pāṭumō tōzhi?
rāvintoṭukkatte yāmattileṅkilum
pōrātirikkumō tōzhī
kaṇṇaninnenne maṛakkumō tōzhī?

Friend, will Kanna come today? Will He sing with His friends? My dear comrade, won't He come at least at the end of the night? Friend, will Kanna forget me?

kāṇmatundō sakhi dureduretteṇgān
kāṛoḷivarṇṇante kāmyakaḷēbaram?
kēḷppatundō sakhi ā muḷantandil
ninnōlunna nāda vṛndāvana sārangi?

Friend, can you see somewhere afar the enchanting form of the cloud colored boy? O my friend, are you hearing the soul stirring music emanating from His flute?

ī virahattinte tāpam sahiykkāten
prāṇa sañchāram nilacchupōmō sakhi?
tāmarasāṣa niṇgettunna nēramī
rādhayillāteyāyālō priya sakhī?

O my companion, will my life breath stop, unable to bear the pangs of separation? My dear friend, when that lotus eyed One comes, what will happen if this Radha is no more?

illa sakhī, varum kaṇṇan varum - ninte
kaṇṇunīrin vila naṣtamāvilleṭō
rādhayillēl pinneyā muḷantandile
nādalahari nilaykkumennōrkka nī

No, friend, Kanna will surely come. You are not going to lose the value of your tears! Know that in the absence of Radha, no enchanting music will emanate from that bamboo reed!

KAṆṆĀ VĀDĀ UṆṆI

kaṇṇā vādā uṇṇi kaṇṇā vāṭā

Come, O Kanna (boy Krishna), come charming

Kanna!veṇṇa kaṭṭuṇṇānāyi kaṇṇā vāṭā

Come, Kanna, feed Yourself on stolen butter!

āṭānayi pāṭānayi kaṇṇā vāṭā

Come Kanna, to sing and dance!

gōkkaḷe mēykkānāyi kaṇṇā vāṭa

Come Kanna, to graze the cows!

carattaṇyānāyi kaṇṇā vāṭā

Come, Kanna, to get a hug!

cāñjādi ceriñjādi kaṇṇā vāṭā

Come Kanna, with hopping and skipping steps!

puñciri tūki nī kaṇṇā vāṭā

Come Kanna, smiling all the way

muraliyil amṛtumāyi kaṇṇā vāṭā

Come Kanna, with nectar flowing out of Your bamboo flute!

pālada tinnānāyi kaṇṇā vāṭā

Come Kanna, to sample some cream!

pāyasamunnānayi kaṇṇā vāṭā

Come Kanna, for a meal of sweet rice pudding!

nanda nandana sundara rūpa
kaṇṇā kārvarna
mānasa cōra maru mukil varṇna
kaṇṇā kārvarna

Kanna, darling of Nanda, handsome one, dark as rain clouds, come, Kanna, come!

KAṆṆUNĪRĀL KAṆṆU

kaṇṇunīrāl kaṇṇu kāṇātirunnāl
kaṇṇan varumbōḷ nī entōnnu ceyyum
kaṇṇe karayāte nī kāttirikkû
kaṇṇan varum vare kaṇṇīratakkû

O eyes always filled with tears, when Kannan comes, how will you see Him? Please wait for Him without crying and control your tears until He arrives.

kaṇṇunīrellām karaññu kaḷaññāl
kaṇṇante pādābhiṣēkam muṭaṅgum
kaṇṇan trikanu kondu ninne tazhukum
annu nī ānandakaṇṇīr pozhikku

If all the tears are gone, the washing of Kannan's feet won't be carried out; when He compassionately glances at you, at that time you can shed tears of joy or bliss.

kaṇṇane dūrattu kandāluṭane
kaṇṇe nī cenniṅgetirēttiṭēṇam
ennu varum kaṇṇanennaṟiyīla
kaṇṇe nī kaṇṇima cimmātirikkū

When you see Him at a distance, O eyes, you should run and welcome Him. When He will come is not known, but without blinking, you should watch and wait for Him.

kaṇṇan mazhamukil varṇṇan varumbōḷ
enne kuṟicchonnu nī uṇarttallē
kaṇṇe nī kaṇṇane kandeṭuttuḷḷin
kaṇṇilēkkānayichenne uṇarttû

When the cloud colored Kannan comes, please don't tell anything about me. O eyes, you just lead him to the inner eyes and then let me be awakened.

KAṆṆU NĪRĀL ÑĀN AMMĒ

kaṇṇu nīrāl ñān ammē pādam kazhukīṭām
karuṇāmayī nī cārattan aññiṭumō?
kadanattāleriyunnu ninnil aliññiṭām
kanivamṛtaruḷiṭānanaññīṭumō? iniyum
viḷambam arutenteyammē

When I wash Your blessed feet with my tears, Amma, the embodiment of compassion, will You come to me? My mind is burning with sorrow in order to merge in You. Will You come to shower the nectar of mercy? My Mother, don't delay any more.

janmāntaraṅgaliḷ alaññu naṭannu ñān
nin tiru kazhalil aṇaññīṭāte
māyāgarttattil patikkuṇōrennil
kṛipa coriyēṇamen jagadambikē iniyum
viḷambam arutenteyammē

Without merging in Your blessed feet, I have roamed about in various births. My Universal Mother, have mercy on this poor soul who is about to fall in the false pit of illusion. My Mother, don't delay any more.

pizhakaḷadhikamāyi ceytirikkām ñān
piriyarutē! ammē! veṭiyarutē!
piṭayunna manassin kadanaṅgaḷakattān
viḷambam arutente jagadambikē iniyum
vilambam arutenteyammē

I might have made so many mistakes. Still, Amma, You should not leave me! To remove the sorrows of my trembling mind, don't delay, my Universal Mother, don't delay any more, my Universal Mother.

KAṆṆUNĪR TŌRĀTTA

kaṇṇunīr tōrātta rāvukaḷ etra pōyi
innum varān kanivillē dayānidhē
ōrō nimiṣavum ōrō yugāntyamāyi
tīmazha peytu peytettunnu śrīdharā

How many nights have I passed with my eyes overflowing with tears? O Compassionate One, won't Thou kindly come even today? O Sreedhara Krishna, to me each moment seems to be an aeon of fiery showers.

koḷḷimīn vāḷiḷakkīṭum niśakaḷil
nin puṟappāṭenu kāṭṭu karaññu ñān
kūriruḷettikkum ōrō svarattilum
nin varavenna pratīkṣayil ñeṭṭi ñān

Thinking that the swirling swords of lightning indicate Thy pageantry, I wait for Thee all through the nights. Expecting Thy footsteps at each of the undertones brought in by the darkness, I remain.

kaṇṇā nirāmaya prēmārdra mānasā
nin mṛdu hāsamin ennu ñān kandiṭum
viṅgi viṅgikkeṇu kaṇṇīril muṅgumī
dāsiye kāttiṭān enniṅgu vanniṭum

O Kanna, ever free from sorrow, Whose heart is softened by love, when will I be able to see Thy mellow smile? When will Thou come to save this sobbing, weeping maid who is drowning in her tears?

ninvazhi tārayil pullāyi muḷaikkuvān
maṇtariyākān anugrahikkenne nī
alleṅkil nin bhakta dāsar pūśīṭunna
candanattin kaṇa mākkanē mādhava

Bless me to be reborn as grass or a grain of sand on Thy path. Otherwise, make me, O Madhava Krishna, a speck of the sandalwood paste to be smeared by the servants of Thy devotees.

KĀṚALA MĀLA IRUNDUKŪṬI (RĀDHĒ ŚYĀM BŌLŌ)

rādhē śyām bōlō rādhē rādhē śyām (3x)
bōlō rādhē śyām bōlō rādhē śyām rādhē śyām

kāṛala māla irundukūṭi
mānasa vāniṭamāke mūṭi
kaṇṇan sadā varṣameghamāti
rādhā manōvāniyāke mūṭi

The sky of the mind became fully covered by the accumulation of clouds. Kanna, by becoming rain clouds, fully covered Radha's mind, too.

kaṇṇane kāttu karaññu rādha
kaṇṇunīr rāvukaḷ peytu ninnu
kaṇṇā nī eṅgupōyi eṅgupōyi
ennātma nāyakan eṅgupōyi

Radha wept in expectation of Kanna. The nights poured out tears! Kanna, where have You gone? Where has gone the heart of my soul?

vīndum taḷirttu pūttī vanaṅgaḷ
kāḷindi pāṭittuṭichiṭunnu
pūnilāvetti pūmtennaletti
nī mātramentē varāññu kaṇṇā?

These forests have flourished again. River Kalindi sings and dances. Moonlight has spread, the breeze is blowing. Still, Kanna, why are You alone not coming?

madhumāsam pōyi śarattu pōyi
etra ṛitukkaḷ kozhiññu pōyi

pūkal kozhiññu maram kozhiññu
kaṇṇan kṛpayum kozhiññu pōyō?

The sweet month has gone. Also, the autumn season is over. How many seasons passed by? Flowers and trees dropped down. Has Kanna's mercy also passed away?

KARAYĀTE KARAYUNNA

karayāte karayunna vṛndāvanī ninte
karaḷinte nombaram āraṛiññu
uraceyyuvī rādhā varumiṅgu mādhavan
madhurayā gōpannu rasamāyiṭā

O Vrindavani, who knows Your heartaches, who is crying without crying? This Radha is saying that Madhavan will come back. That cowherd boy won't like Mathura.

uṇaru vṛndāvanī calanamattiṅgane
maravichu nī kiṭannīṭarute
eviṭe ninnullāsa bhaṅgikaḷ sarvatum
karutaṇē kaṇṇan mataṅgītumē

O Vrindavani, wake up. You should not lie down like this as if paralyzed, without any movement. Where is Your festive beauty? You should keep everything, as Kannan will surely return.

eviṭe nin pūnilā puñciri saurabam
coriyumā pūkkalum kuḷirttennalum
eviṭeyā kāḷindi tan kaḷanisvanam
eviṭeyā kiḷikaḷtan kaḷakūjanam?

Where are Your moonlight smile, sweet smelling flowers, and breeze? Where is the sweet sound of Kalindi? Where is the humming of birds?

vṛndāvanattine kutāṭe kaṇṇanu
sukhameṅgumalpavum kiṭṭukilla
gōpikaḷ gōkaḷum gōparum rādhayum
illāte mādhavan vāzhukilla

Without Vrindavan, Kanna won't get any happiness anywhere. Madhavan won't live without the Gopis, Gopas, cows and Radha.

madhurāpurikkoru madhurāvumillennu
madhuripu vekkam manassilākkum
karayumī rādhayē, vṛndāvanattine
kāṇuvān kaṇṇaniṅgettumallō

The killer of the demon Madhu will easily recognize the fact that Mathurapuri is not at all sweet. Kannan will come back to see this weeping Radha and Vrindavan!

KĀṚOḶI CANDRAN

kāṛoḷi candran maṛañña śēṣam
kaṇṇan madhuraykku pōya śēṣam
śrī rādhā mōham kalarnnu māzhki
kaṇṇīril muṅgippaticchu maṇṇīl

After the cloud complexioned moon has vanished, after Kannan has gone to Madhura, Sri Radha wept bitterly due to passionate attachment. She fell on the ground immersed in tears.

kṛṣṇane cinticchu kṛṣṇa bhāvam
pūndorā rādha piṭaññeṇīttu
kātara bhāvatilaṅumiṅgum
nōkki nōkki kaṇṇīrozhukki

By constant thought of Krishna, She Herself became Krishna and getting up quickly, looked here and there with a sorrowful face and began weeping.

eṅgu pōyen priya tōzhi rādha
vayyī viraham sahicchīṭuvān
ñān vallavākkum kaṭuttu connō
mattoru gōpiye nōkkiyennō

"Where has my dear friend Radha gone? I can't bear this separation anymore. Have I said any harsh word to Her or have I looked at another Gopi?

tōzhī viḷicchīṭū rādhikaye
rādhayillātilla kṛṣṇaneṅgum
kṛṣṇanum rādhayum vēṟēyāṇō
rādhayum kṛṣṇanum veriṭāmō

"Friend, call Radhika. Without Radha there won't be Krishna. Are Krishna and Radha separate? Can Radha and Krishna separate?"

kṛṣṇane cinticchu kṛṣṇa bhāvam
pūndorā rādha naṭannu nīṅgi
pinneyō bōdham teḷiññanēram
kṛṣṇa kṛṣṇēti kuzhaññu vīṇu

By constant thought of Krishna, Radha got Krishna bhava. In that bhava, She began walking. When She became conscious, she fell down chanting "Krishna, Krishna."

rādhē śyām śrī hari rādhē śyām
rādhē rādhē śrī hari rādhē rādhē

KARUṆĀMAYĪ DĒVĪ

karuṇāmayī dēvī kai tozhunnitā nin
kāruṇyāmṛitattinnāyi kai tozhunnitā
kazhaliṇa kūppunnōr agatikaḷ ñaṅgaḷil
kāruṇya mēkuvānāyi kai tozhunnitā - ammē

O Compassionate Goddess, we salute You with joined palms, we salute You for Your nectarean compassion. We prostrate at Your Feet that Your compassion may fall on us.

ajñāna kūriruṭṭil peṭṭu pōyi ñaṅgaḷ
vijñāna dīpam kāttān kai tozhunnitā
ānanda rūpiṇi amṛtēśvari dēvī
kāruṇyāmṛitattinnāyi kai tozhunnitā

We are lost in the pitch darkness of nescience. We salute You with joined palms, O blissful Goddess Amriteswari, we salute You for the Light of Your Knowledge, we salute You for Your nectarean compassion.

kāmādikaḷḷām mālinyamakaluvān
kāruṇnya mūrtti tan adimalar vanaṅgunnu
snēha svarūpiṇi amṛitēśvari dēvi
kāruṇyāmṛitattinnāyi kai tozhunnitā

We bow down to Your holy Feet, O Goddess Amriteswari, Compassion Incarnate, full of Love, we bow down to rid ourselves of all impurities like lust and anger. We salute You for Your nectarean compassion.

KARUṆĀMAYI NĪ KṚPĀMAYĪ NĪ

karuṇāmayi nī kṛpāmayī nī
vijñānamayī ānandamayī ammā

amṛtānandamayī jananī amṛtānandamayī

O Mother Amritanandamayi, Thou art the embodiment of compassion, grace, knowledge, and bliss.

vighnavināśinī vināyaka jananī
divyamayī ammā vidyāmayī
buddhī pradāyinī vēda svarūpiṇī
bōdhamayī ammā satcinmayī ammā
amṛtānandamayī

O Mother, Destroyer of obstacles, Mother of Ganesha, Embodiment of Divinity and Supreme Knowledge, O Mother, Bestower of Wisdom, Thou art the very essence of the Vedas, Pure Awareness Absolute, Existence and Knowledge Absolute.

pustaka dhāriṇi vīṇāpāṇī brahmasvarūpiṇī
sarasvatī
dēvī mahā lakṣmī pārvatī śaṅkarī
ādī parā śaktī jagadambikē ammāamṛtānandamayī

O Sarasvati, holding the sacred book (Vedas) in one hand and the veena in the other, Thou art the very embodiment of the Supreme Being.

brahmamayī ammā viṣṇūmayī
śaktīmayī śiva śaktīmayī
śrī kṛṣṇa bhāvamāyi parā śaktī bhāvamāyi
kāttaruḷēṇam jagadambikē
ammāamṛitānandamayī

Appearing in Thy two divine moods of Sri Krishna and Devi, bless me, O Mother of the Universe, Amritanandamayi.

KARUṆĀRDRAMĀNASAN

karuṇārdramānasan kadanārtti nāśakan
kamaniya vigrahan pōyi maṛaññu
karakāṇā kaṭalilī ezhakaḷ vīzhuvān
aparādhamentiṅgu ceytu śaure

The One whose mind is full of compassion, the One who removes all sorrows, the One who has enchanting features has gone! What wrong have these poor ones done to fall in the shoreless ocean?

oru nāḷum piriyilla praṇayakulekṣaṇan
eritīyil namme eṛiyukilla
sakalatum avanāyiṭṭaṭiyara vechallō
śaranāgatarkkavan tunayallayō

That affectionate-eyed One will never leave us. He will never throw us in burning fire. Haven't we surrendered everything unto Him? Is He not a companion to those who have surrendered?

oru pōḷa kaṇṇatacchīṭilla mādhavan
karayātirikkilla nammēyorttu
muraliyil madhurāga madhutûkumā sakhan
kaṭhinanākānoṭṭum vazhiyumilla

Madhavan won't be having even a wink of sleep. He would have cried on remembering us. Is He not our friend who used to pour out nectarous music through His flute? It is unlikely that He is hard-hearted.

karuṇā nidhē rādha prāṇan dharippatō
tava darśanārtha maṇōrttiṭane
oru noṭṭamoru hāsam nalkaṇē atināyi
ttoru kōṭi janmaṅgaḷ tapamirikkam

Oh, Embodiment of Compassion, know that Radha lives only for Your vision. Glance at me once, give me one smile. For that I can do tapas for ten million births.

KARUṆAYILLĒ AMMĒ

karuṇayillē ammē karunayillē
kanivin poruḷē kanivillē ammē

O Mother, don't You have any compassion? O Kindness Incarnate, where is Your kindness?

kālam munnōṭṭozhukunnu
khēdam tiṅgi perukunnu

Time flows forward ceaselessly, and my sorrow is building up to its fullness.

iniyum darśanam ēkān ammē
bhāvamillē ammē bhāvamillē

Don't you have any intention of granting me Your darshan yet?

cārattaṇayān vaikunnō
en kaṇṇāl ninne kāṇṇillē

Why the delay to come close to me? Will I never see You with these eyes of mine?

ennuṭe amma nīyallē
paital ivan [ivaḷ] nin makanallē [makaḷallē]

Aren't You my own Mother, and this infant, isn't he (she) Your own son (daughter)?

KAṬṬITTAYIR TARĀM

kaṭṭittayir tarām kācchiya pāl tarām
kuṭṭanorummayum amma tarām
taṭṭi vīzhāte nī muṭṭukālāl tuzha
ññoṭṭenṭatuttu vā muttam tarām

I will offer You thick yogurt, sweet boiled milk, and a sweet kiss. Come to me on Your knees without stumbling on the way and Your Mother will again kiss You.

poṭṭiyaraññāṇam mātti tarām-mañña
paṭṭunul kōṇakam keṭṭi tarām
kaṭṭi veṇṇa tarām puttanavil tarām
taṭṭam niṛaye pāl cōru tarām

I will give You a new waist-belt and new silk shawl. I have butter, fresh flattened rice, and a whole plate full of pudding.

ōmana paitalē oṭakkuzhal tarām
ōmana cundil tēn tēchu tarām
venmuttu mālakaḷ cārttittarā māṛil
kaṇmaṇi nīyente cāre varû

O my dear one, I shall give You a flute, honey, and lots of pearl necklaces on Your chest, please come near me.

atta mayil pīli mātti niṛukayil
mattoru ponpīli cārtti tarām
muṭṭattiḷaveyil muṭṭi viḷikkunnu
kattakkiṭāvē nī kaṇturakkū

I will remember Your old peacock feather and replace it with a new golden peacock feather. O my darling, the morning sun is already shining; please open Your eyes.

kēṭṭalumōmanē vīṭṭinte kōlāyil
caṭṭattorūññāl ñān keṭṭi tarām
kuṭṭittam māṟiyāl muttatte tēnmāvil
kaṭṭāyam valyūññāliṭṭu tarām

Please listen my dear, I will hang a new swing on our veranda for You. When You grow up, I will put a bigger swing on the mango tree in our yard.

muṭṭanuññālenikkiṭṭu tarika - ñān
kuṭṭiyallottiri muṭṭanāyi
ēṭṭaninnum kochu kuṭṭiyāṇamme ñān
ēṭṭanekkāḷitā nīṭṭam vechu

O Mother, I am not small any more; please have the bigger swing hung for Me. I am grown up. Elder brother is still small; look, I am taller than he.

kaṇṇā nī kaḷḷanāṇamma kandaṇṇente
pinnil nī pīṭhattil poṅgi nilppū
kaṇṇā teḷiyēnda pīṭham veṭiyukil
aṇṇante tōḷōḷam nīḷam varām

O Kanna, You are a liar. I can see You standing on a stool. If the stool is removed, You are only up to Your brother's shoulder!

KĀYĀMBŪVARṆṆA VARIKA

kāyāmbūvarṇṇā varika nī kaṇṇā
karaḷinu kavita nī kārvarnā - kaṇṇā

O Krishna, You who have the complexion of a "Kayambu" flower (a deep blue-colored flower), come. O Kanna (childhood name of Krishna), You are the song of my heart.

rādhā mādhava rāsavilōlā rāgavilōla harē
muralī dhara manamōhana kṛṣṇā
munijana pāla harē

manamayil nin nava mukiloḷi tēṭi
mathi maṛannāṭunnu mada bhara kēḷi
mathi mukhi vadhu rādha mazhavillāyī
mukiloḷi maṇivarṇṇa nin kuḷir māṭil
rādhā mādhava

My mind, the peacock, seeking Your new cloud-like hue, dances in exaltation, forgetting itself. Your consort, Radha, the moon-faced one, shines like a rainbow as she lies on Your cool chest, O Krishna, my dark-complexioned jewel.

madhumasa maṇarikaḷ viṭarna vṛdāvanam
madabhara muraḷī gāna vimōhanam
madhura nilāvarṇi maṭu malaraṇi kuñjam
tava naṭa nōtsava surabhila rangam
rādha mādhava

Vrindavan with its fully blossomed flowers in spring is enchanting with the exalting songs of Your flute. The sweet flowery creepers intertwine in the light of the full moon, setting the fragrant stage for Your festive dance.

mama manam oru pūjā maṭumalar kaṇṇā
tava pada taḷir cūṭi nirupama bhangī
mati varuvōḷavum mana mayilēṛi
vihāra murāri hṛdaya vihāri
rādha mādhava

My mind becomes a blossoming flower to be offered for worship as it falls at Your tender feet of incomparable beauty, O Kanna. O Indweller of my heart, Murari (Krishna), let me ascend the peacock of my mind and revel in You.

KĀYĀ PĪYA SUKH SE SŌYĀ

kāyā pīya sukh se sōyā
nā hakka jān na magavāyyā
kamala mukha
rāma bhajana kō diyā

We eat, drink, and sleep comfortably, but we never sing about the lotus-faced Rama.

jā mukha nīsādīna rāma nāma nahi
ō mukha katchu na kiyā
kamala mukha
rāma bhajana kō diyā

The name of Rama never seems to come from our mouths. O mouth, why aren't you singing the songs of the lotus-faced Rama?

laka chorāsi tere pira dhara
sundara tanu magavāyā
kamala mukha
rāma bhajana kō diyā

Our eyes are not seeing the Lord's beautiful form, and we never sing about the lotus-faced Rama.

kaha ta kabīra suno bāyi sādhō
āya vaisā gayā
kamala mukha
rāma bhajana kō diyā

We come and we go but we never sing the devotional songs of the lotus-faced Rama. Kabir is saying, "O listen brother sadhus, sing the devotional songs of the lotus-faced Rama."

KRISHNA GŌVINDA GŌPĀLA

śrī kṛṣṇa gōvinda gōpāla
hari gōvinda gōvinda gopālā
śrī kṛṣṇa gōvinda
murali manōhara
gōkula nandana gōpāla

kṛṣṇa	Allattractor
gōvinda	Lord of the cows
gōpala	Cowherd
murali	Flute player
hari	Refuge of the distressed
manōhara	Mindravishing
gōkula	Krishna's village
nandana	Son

dēvaki nandana gōpālā
dānava bhañjana gōpāla
śrī kṛṣṇa gōvinda
murali manōhara gōkula nandana gōpālā

dēvaki nandana	Son of Devaki
danava bhañjana	Destroyer of the demons

nandakumāra gōpālā
navanīta cōra gōpālā
śrī kṛṣṇa gōvinda
murali manōhara
gōkula nandana gōpālā

nandakumara	Son of Nanda
navanīta cōra	Butter-thief

gōkula nandana gōpi manōhara
gōvardhanōdhara gōpālā
gōkula nandana gōpālā
gōvardhanōdhara gōpālā

gōpi manōhara	Enchanter of the Gopis minds
gōvardhanōdhara	Holder of the Govardhana Hill

KṚṢṆA GŌVINDA

kṛṣṇa gōvinda gōvinda gōpālā
kṛṣṇa murali manōhara nanda lālā

kṛṣṇa	The Allattractor
gōvinda	Lord of the cows
gōpala	Cowherd boy
murali	Flute player
manōhara	Enchanter of the mind
nandalala	Son of Nanda

KṚṢṆA JINKA NĀM HE

kṛṣṇa jinka nām hē
gōkula jinka dhām hē
aise śrī bhagavān kō
bāram bār praṇām hē

O Krishna, Who lives in Gokul, to such a Lord, I bow to You again and again.

yaśōda jinkī māyyā hē
nandaji bapayya hē
aise srī gopāl kō
bāram bār praṇām hē

Whose mother is Yashoda, whose father is Nanda, to that cowherd boy, I bow again and again.

lūt lūt dadhi makhana khāyo
bāl bāl sang denu curāyo
aise līla dhām kō
bāram bār praṇām he

Who used to steal yogurt and butter along with other children, Who disposed of the demon Denu, to that One Who abides in His Eternal Play, I bow again and again.

drūpada sutā kilācha bachāyo
grāhise gajiko bhanda cudāyo
aise śrī bhagavān kō
bāram bār praṇām hē

Who saved the son of Drupada Kilacha, Who separated the Elephant from the Alligator, I bow down to that Lord again and again.

KṚṢṆA MANA MŌHANĀ

kṛṣṇa kṛṣṇa mana mōhanā
citta cōra rādhā jīvanā
mēgha śyāma madhūsūdanā
rādhā kānta yadū nandanā

O Krishna, Enchanter of the mind, Stealer of the mind, the very life of Radha, Who is dark as a cloud, Who killed the demon Madhu, Beloved of Radha, Descendant of Yadu!

KṚṢṆĀ MUKUNDĀ

kṛṣṇā mukundā mādhavā
madhusūdanā muralīdharā
manasija mōhana
sarasijānana śrī

O Krishna, Bestower of Liberation, Goddess Lakshmi's Consort, Slayer of the demon Madhu, Holder of the flute, lotus-eyed Lord, You enchant our heart with Your beauty.

nanda nandanā nanda sundarā
santatānanda tē namāmyaham
santatam sukritātma sundara
vandanam krama mukti dāyakā

O Nanda's Darling, Essence of happiness and beauty. O Source of perpetual bliss, I prostate before You. O perpetual essence of all goodness, O Beautiful One, I worship Thee, the Bestower of eternal salvation.

nitānta ramyā sarōja nētra
nirāmaya gati tvam ēva dēva
nijān tavāmghri sarōjamāśrayam
kṛpāmṛtam kuru
nirantaram hṛdi

O Abode of perpetual bliss, O lotus-eyed one, O God without even the tiniest flaw, You are my only recourse. Please make Your lotus feet my only resort and shower constantly the nectar of Your Grace in my heart.

KṚṢṆAM VANDĒ

kṛṣṇam vandē jagatgurum
bōlō jai jai jai gōpī śrī kṛṣṇa

I prostrate to Krishna, the Guru of the whole universe. Let us chant: Victory to Krishna, the Beloved of the Gopis.

dēvakī tanayam yaśōda bālam
rādhā vilōlam mānasa cōram

He is the son of Devaki, the boy of Yasoda; He is the Enchanter who steals devotees' hearts.

vēdānta sāram gītōpadēśam (3x)
pūrṇāvatāram kṛṣṇa gōpālam
sādhu samrakṣakam rādhē gōpālam

Krishna's message, the Gita, is the quintessence of the Vedas. He is the complete, full incarnation who protects sages and the downtrodden and He is Radha-Gopal.

LALITA LALITA ŚRĪ LALITA

lalita lalita śrī lalita
lalita lalita jagan mātā

viśva vimōhini śiva lalita
lalita lalita jagan mātā

vēda vilāsini śiva lalita
lalita lalita jagan mātā

mukti pradāyini śiva lalita
lalita lalita jagan mātā

lalita	Playful Goddess

jagan mātā	Mother of the World
viśva vimōhini	Enchantress of the Universe
śiva lalita	Lord Shiva's Lalita
vēda vilāsini	Who manifests as the Veda
mukti pradāyini	Giver of Liberation

MAHĀKĀLI JAGADŌ DHĀRIṆI

mahākāli jagadō dhāriṇi
hē pralayaṅkari hē abhayankari
jāgō pralayaṅkari manamōhini

O Mahakali, You sustain the whole Universe and also destroy it. O Giver of solace, You captivate my mind. Please awake and cast Your glance at this person.

muktikēśini muṇḍamālinī
katakahastini dukhanivāriṇi
kāli kapālini trilōka pālini
jāgō pralayaṅkari manamōhini

O Bearer of salvation, Wearer of a necklace of skulls, Giver of boons, O Protector of the three worlds, Please awake and also cast Your glance at this person. Destroyer of evil, O Kali, You captivate my mind.

brahma viṣṇu nārada pūjē
śaṅkara tava caraṇōm mē virāje
vāsana anāvṛta hē aparājita
jāgō pralayaṅkari manamōhini

Brahma, Vishnu, and Narada are continuously worshipping You. Śankara always resides at Your feet. You are eternally victorious and untouched by vasanas. You captivate my mind. Please awake and cast Your glance at this person.

MAMA JANANĪ BHUVANĀ

mama jananī bhuvanāmaya śamanē
kamala dalāyata nayanē
tribhuvana mōhana vadanē mama hṛdi
maruvuka manasukha dhanamē

O my Mother, Your face enchants the three worlds and Your eyes bring to mind the beauty of a lotus petal. You loosen the shackles of all creatures. You are the priceless wealth that gives comfort to our minds. Please abide in my heart.

sudhanya sundara surabhila cintā
malaritalāl abhiṣēkam ceyyām
praṇava svarāmṛita gāna vilōlē
kanivin āmṛtārnavamē

I offer You this worship using flower petals from my mind. I offer these to You, who are the very embodiment of nectarean kindness, and who are enraptured in music that is permeated by the sound OM.

madhu maya rūpiṇi mangala dāyiṇi
mana sukha dāna suśīlē
sahṛdaya hṛdaya sulālita caraṇē
maruvuka mama mana malaril

O You of beauteous form, Bestower of auspiciousness, who delights in making the gift of mental peace, and are the presiding deity in the hearts of Her devotees, please abide in my mind.

MANASSIL VARṆṆAPPOLI

manassil varṇṇappolimakaḷēttum
anaśvara gāyikayallō
mananam ceyyum manamatilennum
naṭanam ceyavavaḷallō

vazhiyil kallukaḷ mullukaḷ nīkki
niratti veṭippu varutti
mizhiyil neyttiri dīpavumāyi nin
varavum kāttu vasippu

Are You not the Eternal Singer who produces colorful presents to our minds? Are You not the one who dances in the contemplative mind?

nin virahāgniśaraṅgaḷorāyiram
uḷḷu tuḷaññu taṛaññu
sandhyā mlānata pōle manassil
aliññu viṣādamuṛaññu

cambaka sūnasugandha parāgam
tûvumilam tennal pōl
āgatamāvuka svāgatamōtu-
nāgama saundaryamē nī

Thousands of arrows of separation from You pierced my inner being and got stuck. The sorrow got condensed in my mind like the weariness of the dusk.

eriññutāzhum tārakamāyi mizhi
kuzhaññu vīhum mumbē
karaḷinnita vazhi karinizhal tīṅgi
aṭaññu mūṭum mumbē

Don't let my eyes faint and fall like a falling star. Don't block the narrow door to my mind by black shadows.

ēkuka nin karuṇāmṛtarūpa
manōhara driśya muhûrttam
mēvuka hṛdi mazhamēgham māññoru
mānattambiḷi pōle ammē ammē

Give the glorious moment of seeing Your enchanting, compassionate form. Shine forth in my heart like the moon in a sky devoid of clouds.

MĀNAVA HṚDAYATTIN

mānava hṛdayattin māyā maṛa nīkki
teḷiyunna nānmarakkātalē
mānasamambayil marātirutti ñān
dhyāna nilīnam vasippū ammē

O Mother, You are the Light that shines in the human heart, when the veil of Maya is lifted. Please let me focus my mind entirely on You, and remain immersed in that meditation.

nirvāṇa śānti tan nirvṛti āṇu nī
nirmala hṛdayattil amṛta svarūpiṇī
mānava jīvita pātayil neyttiri
nālam teḷippū nī nīḷe nīḷe (mānava)

You are the essence of the peace of Nirvana, reposing in the human heart like sweet nectar. You illumine the path of human destiny.

vandichiṭunnōrum nindichiṭunnōrum
anyarallā ammaykkaruma makkaḷ
ellārkkum ammayāyi, ellārilum tulya
bhāvattil tūkunnu snēhāmṛtam (mānava)

Those who salute You and those who insult You are the same to You — they are all Your dear children. You shower the nectar of Love equally on all, and abide as the Mother of all.

MAṆYŪKAL MŪTUM

maṇyūkal mūtum mānam mele
ī pampayitozhukum tīram tāzhe
ī kānanaṅgaliḷūṭe varunnu ninne kandītān
ñaṅgaṭe cundil ūri varunnu svāmiye ayyappō

Mist covers the sky above and the land through which the Pampa River flows below. We come through these forests to see You, and the words "Svamiye Ayyappo" trickle through our lips.

svāmiye ayyappō ayyappō svāmiye!

Ayyappa, You are my Lord! O Prince of Pandala, You who use the great leopard as Your vehicle, we come to reach Your abode.

dūrattōru mala tannil celottū vasikkunnā
svāmi ninnuṭe rūpam kānān
ñaṅgaḷ tēṭi varunnunde
ī ñaṅgaḷ tēṭi varunnunde

Svami (Lord), You Who gracefully abide on a mountain far away, we come in search of You, we come in search of You.

āyiram dīpangal āyiram dīpangal
onnichu minnunnā puṇya sthalam
pampa ārinṭe tīrame puṇya sthalam

A thousand lamps! A thousand lamps shine together on the holy shores of the Pampa River. This indeed is a sacred land, a holy land.

svāmiye ayyappō ayyappō svāmiye!
pandala nandanane svāmiye ayyappō
van puli vāhanane svāmiye ayyappō!
nin savidham manayu vānāyi ñaṅgaḷ vārunnu
ñaṅgaṭe cundil ūri varunnu svāmiye ayyappō

Ayyappa, You are my Lord! O Prince of Pandala, You Who use the great leopard as Your vehicle, we come to reach Your abode.

manyūkal mūtam mānam mēle
svāmiye ayyappō ayyapō svāmiye
svāmi śaraṇam ayyappa śaraṇam

Lord Ayyappa! Lord Ayyappa! You are my refuge and You are my Lord.

MAYAṄGUNNA PAKALINNU

mayaṅgunna pakalinnu tanalēki nī ī
makaninnu mayaṅgunnoriṭamētammā
malarinnu niṟamēki maṇamēki nī ī
makanamma dukhattī kanalēkiyō? (2x)

You have given shelter to the dozing day. Amma, where should this son sleep? You have given color and fragrance to flowers. Why did You give the charcoal of sorrow to Your son?

ulakinnu mazhayēki veyilēki nī atil
maruvunna manujarkku madamēki nī

pakalōnu nirakānti katirēki nī mama
hṛdayattin avirāmamirulēkiyō ammē

You have given showers and sunlight to the world and to those who are residing in this world You have given lust also. You have given bright shining rays to the sun. Why have You given continuous darkness to my heart?

pavanante tanuvinnu taṇalēki nī ente
hṛdayattin azhalinte veyilēki nī
kazhaltārilabhayam nalku vatennahō mama
mizhimunnil teḷiyunna dinamennaho? ammē (2x)
niramizhi teḷiyunna dinamennaho?

You made the body of the wind cool, but made my heart hot by giving me unending hardships. When are You going to give me shelter at Your blessed feet? Also, on which day will You shine in front of my eyes?

MĒRĒ PRABHU TU MUJHKŌ

mērē prabhu tu mujhkō batā
tērē sivā mekyā karum
tērī śaran kō cōd kar
jag kī śaran kō kyā karum

O my Lord, please tell me what I will do without You? Giving up Your refuge, what will I do by taking refuge in the world?

candramā banke āp hi
tārōm me jag magā rahē
tērī camak kē sāmne
dīpak jalā kē kyā karum

You shine as the light in the moon and twinkling stars. What is the use of waving a light before Your effulgence?

kaliyōm me basa rahē hō tum
phūlōm me hasa rahē hō tum
mērē tō man me vō base
mandir me jāke kyā karum

You are the life in tiny buds; You smile in blossoming flowers. You are in my heart, so what will I gain by going to a temple?

banke bramar āp hi
phūlōm me gun gunā rahē
sundar sangīt ke sāmne
kīrtan sunā ke kyā karum

You are a bee humming over the flowers. My singing hymns are no comparison to Your divine music.

bādal me banke indra dhanu
khuda hī jagat sajā rahē
candan apī hō hōlikā
tuch par cadā kē kyā karum

As a rainbow among the clouds, You are decorating the world. Can I lend any glory to You by applying sandalwood paste?

MILNĀ TUJHE MAI CĀHU

milnā tujhe mai cāhu
kaise mai tujhese milu
kōyī bhakta jenōmse pūchē
ammā kō kaise bhule

I want to be with You. Please tell me what I should do. Ask the devotees if they will ever forget Amma.

śakti jo banke baithi
bhaktōm ki ānkho mai
dilse yā drishtiyōm se
ammā bhūlengi kaise

She is the power of vision in the eyes of devotees. Can devotees ever keep their eyes and mind away from Amma?

catak jo banke baitte
ammā ki rāha dhekhe
sāgar ke jaise ammā
sabko bhūlengi kaise

Devotees wait for Amma's arrival like the chatak bird waits for rain. Amma is the Ocean of Mercy. Amma will never forget anyone.

suni madhuri bansi
bāvari banke āyi
kahō kṛṣṇa kē hṛday ki
amṛtē bhūlengi kaise

Hearing the sweet tune of the flute I have come here. Can one ever resist the Divine Nectar of Krishna's Love.

MUKUNDA MURĀRI GŌPĀLA

mukunda murāri gōpāla
gōpāla hari gōpāla
murahara giridhara gōpāla
naṭavara sundara gōpāla
gōpāla hari gōpāla

mukunda	Bestower of Liberation
murari	Destroyer of the demon Mura
gōpala	Cowherd boy

hari	Reliever of distress
murahara	Destroyer of Mura
giridhara	Who lifted the mountain
naṭavara sundara	Beautiful dancer

MUNNAMORĀYIRAM

munnamorāyiram janma meṭuttu nī
mannitil dharma ratham teḷichu
nin svēta vastrāñcalattil piṭichu ñān
annokke ninne anugamichū

By taking thousands of incarnations in the past, You have driven the chariot of virtue in this world. Holding the end of Your white robe, I have followed You on all such incarnations.

koñci kuzhaññum kiṇungi karaññum
pinaṅgippiriññum karam grahichum
innum nin kālchuvattil
izhayunnilam kuruññāṇu ñān ammē

Prattling, clattering, quarrelling and separating, joining together, O Mother, I am still a small baby crawling under Your feet.

snēhamṛduṣmala sārasallāpaṅgaḷ
cettassilānanda nirvṛtti dhārakaḷ
jñānārka bhāsal prabhātam teḷippû nin
tūmandahāsa prasannānanam hṛdi

Your soft, warm and loving talks bring rapturous bliss into my heart. Your smiling face shines as the dawn of the sun of knowledge in my heart.

mātṛvātsalyattin mārdavalāḷanam
īṛan nilāvupoluḷḷam tazhukavē
āyiram neyttiri nāḷaṅgaḷāl ninne
ārādhanam ceyvû sādaram ñān sadā

When the soft fondling of Your motherly affection embraces my heart, I humbly worship You with thousands of ghee-wicked lamps.

tenūtumummayum snēha vātsalyavum
ōmal kiṭāṅgaḷkuṇarvu varṣīkke nin
kāruṇya pīyūṣa lōlanetrangaḷil
lōkam kuḷīrttu nilkunnu nirantaram

When Your sweet kiss and loving affection bring awakening to Your darling children, the world of bliss is seen in Your compassionate eyes.

MURALĪ DHARA GŌPĀLA

muralī dhara gōpāla mukundā
muni jana mana haranā
vraja vadhuvōm kē hṛdaya cakōra
madhurā puri sadanā

nanda nandanā navānīta cōrā
manda hāsa vadanā
natana manōhara kisalaya caraṇā
karuṇālaya varadā murali dhara
amara vanditā śyāma śarīrā
pītāmbara vasanā
adhara niyōjita murali manōhara
jagadabhirāma harē murali dhara

makara kundalā malayaja tilakā
mayūra mukuṭa dharā
manda manda hasitānana mōhana
nanda gōpa tanayā
murali dhara

indīvara śyāma sundara nayanā
candra bimba vadanā
trilōka vandita pādāravindā
nirantaram vandē
murali dhara

muralidhara	One who holds the flute
gōpala	The cowherd boy
mukunda	Bestower of salvation
muni janamana harana	The conqueror of the saints minds
vrajavadhuvom kē hṛdayacakōra	The partridge of the heart of the cowherd girls
madhurapuri sadana	One whose house is in Mathura city
nandanandana	The son of Nanda
navanitacōra	The stealer of fresh butter
mandahasavadana	One who has a sweet, smiling face
natanamanōhara	One who dances beautifully
kisalayacaraṇa	One whose feet are like tender leaves
karunalaya varada	The compassionate bestower of boons
amaravandita	Who is worshipped by immortals
śyāmasarīra	One who is darkcomplexioned
pitambaravasana	One who has yellow robes
adhara niyōgita murali manōhara	One who is very charming because he keeps the flute on his lips
jagadabhirama	Who has a worldenchanting form

harē	One who kills his foes
makarakuṇḍala	One having earrings shaped like a fish
malayaja tilaka	One who wears sandalwood paste
mayura mukuṭa dhara	One who has peacock feathers in his crown
mandamanda hasita-nana	Whose face is always lit up with a sweet smile
mōhana	One who attracts
nandagōpa tanaya	The son of Nanda, the cowherd
indivara śyāma sun-dara nayana	One whose eyes are as beautiful as the water lily
candra bimba vadanā	One whose face resembles the full moon
trilōka vanditā pādaravindā	Whose lotus feet are worshipped by the three worlds
nirantaram vandē	I constantly prostrate to Him

MURALI KṚṢṆĀ

murali kṛṣṇā mukunda kṛṣṇā
mōhana kṛṣṇā kṛṣṇā kṛṣṇā
gōpi kṛṣṇā gopāla kṛṣṇā
gōvardhana dhara kṛṣṇā kṛṣṇā

O Krishna, the Flute Player, O Bestower of Liberation, O Enchanting Krishna, O Krishna of the Gopis, Cowherd Krishna, Uplifter of the Govardhana Hill

rādhā kṛṣṇā bāla kṛṣṇā
rāsa vilōlā kṛṣṇā kṛṣṇā
amṛta kṛṣṇā ānanda kṛṣṇā
śrī madhusūdana kṛṣṇā kṛṣṇā

Radha's Krishna, Baby Krishna, Dancer in the Rasa Lila, O Immortal Krishna, Blissful Krishna, O Krishna, the Destroyer of the demon Madhu!

MURALĪ NINADAM KĀTIL

muralī ninadam kātil muzhangān
mazha mukiloli varnnam mizhiyil teḷiyān
karalin kadanakkanalukaḷ anayān
varumō kuvalaya nayanā kṛṣṇā

In order to hear the sound of the flute, to clearly see the color of the cloud, to extinguish the fires of sorrow of the heart, O lotus-eyed Krishna, will You come?

kilukile naṭayum naṛu puñciriyum
karuṇāmṛta rasam ozhukum mizhiyum
karaḷil kaṇikandazhalāṛīṭān
varumō kuvalaya nayanā kṛṣṇā

In order to relieve the pains of my heart, by seeing Your beautiful steps, smile and eyes full of compassion, O lotus-eyed Krishna, will You come?

paramānanda kuḷirala ākum
kaḷa muralīrava svaralaya rāgam
ozhukiyozhukiyen hṛdayataṭākam
niṛayaṇamē kara kaviyaṇamē kṛṣṇā

The melodious music emanating from Your flute will create waves of sweet bliss which will flow continuously to my heart-lake, filling it and overflowing it.

MURALIVĀLE BHAJĀVE

muralivāle bhajāve
murali rasake bhāri
jai muralidhar jai ghana śyām
jai manamōhan rādhe śyām
śyām śyām bōlō
śrī rādhe śyām bōlō

O Holder of the flute, play a melodious tune. Victory to the Holder of the flute, victory to Him Who is blue like the sky, to the Enchanter of the mind, Radha Krishna. Say "Shyam, Shyam"; say "Radhe Shyam."

brahma nāche śankar nāche
nāche suramuni sāre
sūrya candrama dharti nāche
nache nabh ke tāre
o murali sune nārad nāche
kāh gayi hari hari

Brahma dances, Shiva dances, and all the gods and sages dance. The sun, Moon, Earth and the stars also dance to the tune. Hearing the flute, Narada dances and everyone sings "Hari, Hari!"

murali sukar ban ki gāye
dhōdi dhōdi āye
jamuna ji ki chanchal lahare
tirak tirak harghāye
hari darśan ko vyākul gōpi
khōjal simat li

Hearing the flute, everyone came running to the forest. Even the waves of the Yamuna came running to the banks. The Gopis, who were anxious for Krishna's darshan, attained great bliss.

MUTTU MĀRI AMMA

muttu māri amma muttu māri
muttu māri amma muttu māri
devi unnai śaran adāindhom
nēṣa muttu māri

O Mother, Showerer of pearls, O Devi, we have taken refuge in Thee, O loving, affectionate Showerer of pearls.

NĀLAÑCU NĀLEYKKU

nālañcu nāleykku tān jīvitam
nāmeṅgu pōkunnu hē mānavā

This life is only for four or five days. O man, where are you going?

kandinnu kandiṅgu kānāteyāyi
kaṇṇinnu kaṇṇāyatāke maṇṇil

In this world, all your beloved things appear in front of your eyes for some time only. After some time, they disappear.

nīḷunna mōhaṅgal pālunnitā
kāḷunna melaṅgaḷ nāḷamitā

Your endless desires will slide away. See the flames of burning festivities.

entiṅgu bandhaṅgal āru bandhu
māññu pōm mādaka svargga bhangi

What actually is relationship and who is related? All your enchanting heavenly beauties will be wiped away!

śrī mātu pūmātu kāli mātu
kāttu nilkkunnitā svantamamma
ādi mātāvinte pūmaṭiyil
pāṭi mayaṅgitām pūmpaitalē

Here awaits our own Mother. O little baby, you can sleep in the lap of the Eternal Mother while hearing the lullaby.

NAMĀMI KĀLIKE

namāmi kālike praṇāmi kālikē
namāmi kālike praṇāmi santatam
prasīda candikē pracanda candikē
prasīda kālikē praṇāmi santatam

I pray to You with both hands held together, O Kali. I prostrate before You, O Kali. I pray to You with both hands held together, O Kali. I prostrate before You, O Kali. Please shower Your grace on me, O Chandike. O fierce Chandike, shower Your grace on me. O Kalike, I prostrate before You constantly.

namōstu bhairavi raṇōgra bhairavi
namōstu pārvatī praṇāmi santatam
jayōstu maṅgaḷē samastā maṅgaḷē
jayōstu kālikē praṇāmi santatam

I pray to You, O Bhairavi, ferocious in battle with the demons. I pray to You, O Daughter of the Mountain (Himalaya), I prostrate before You constantly. Victory to You, O auspicious One. O eternal, all-pervading Auspiciousness. Victory to You, O Kali. I prostrate before You constantly.

NANDA GŌPAN

nanda gōpan tapamirunnu
sundara kaṇṇan
paṇtorikkal gōkulattil
vannan nāḷinna kaṇṇan janma nāḷinna

The ladies of Gokula say, "Once upon a time Nanda Gopan (Krishna's father) did penance in Gokula and the beautiful Kannan (Krishna) came this day."

ponnin kuṭangaḷil pāl karanna
annannu nalkaṇaṁ nammaḷinna
tālamuzhiyēṇaṁ mamkamārē (2 x)
ālōlaṁ pāṭaṇam ammamārē

"In golden vessel we should collect milk and give it to Kannan. Oh ladies, do arati (worship) to Kannan and, oh mothers, you should clap your hands and sing songs!"

kāḷindiyātil kuḷi kazhiñña
gōpimārelārum nōkki ninnu
āṭakal vāriyoḷiccu kaṇṇan (2x)
ōṭakkuzhalūti ninnu kaṇṇan

"After taking a bath in the Kalindi river the gopis looked for their clothes. But Kannan had taken and hidden them somewhere[4]. And he stood there playing the flute pretending that he knew nothing.

[4] Krishna was only 7 years old when he did this leela to the gopis. It symbolizes stealing the minds of the gopis away from external objects.

NANDAKUMĀRA GŌPĀLĀ

nandakumāra gōpālā -hari-
sundarabāla gōpālā

O Gopala, the son of Nanda, O Gopala, the Handsome Boy the Adorable Child.

naraharirūpa gōpālā
naṭanamanōhara gōpālā
natajanapāla gōpālā
navanitarasika gōpālā

O Gopala, God in human form, O Gopala, the Charming Dancer, O Gopala, the Protector of the humble, O Gopala, the Relisher of fresh butter.

karuṇapūrṇa gōpālā
kamaniya nētra gōpālā
kamsa niṣūdana gōpālā
vasatu sadā hrdi gōpālā

O Gopala, the All Merciful One, O Gopala, with the enticing form, O Gopala, the Slayer of Kamsa, may Thou always reside in my heart.

patitōdhāra gōpālā
paramānanda gōpālā
pāvana caraṇā gōpālā
paripālaya mām gōpālā

O Gopala, the Uplifter of the fallen, O Gopala, the Blissful, O Gopala, Whose Feet are blessed holy, O Gopala, protect and look after me.

NANDALĀL NANDALĀL

nandalāl nandalāl
nandalāl yadu nandalāl
nandalālā navanīta cōrā
rādhā pyāre nandalāl
māyi mīrā mānasa cōrā
hṛdaya vihārā nandalāl

O Son of Nanda, O Son of Nanda, O Son of Nanda, born in the Yadu clan, O Son of Nanda, O Butter-Thief! Beloved of Radha, Son of Nanda, Who stole Mother Mira's mind, That Son of Nanda who plays in the heart.

NANDA LĀLĀ NANDA LĀLĀ

nanda lālā nanda lālā
nandā kē lālā prabhu rādhā lōlā
gōpi lōlā gōpa bālā
citta līlā vilāsa lōlā

O Son of Nanda, O Son of Nanda, For Radha to know joy is to be devoted to the Lord. Soft-hearted toward the Gopis, O Cowherd Boy, My heart is longing for the divine sport of Krishna.

harē rāma harē rāma
rāma rāma harē harē
harē kṛṣṇa harē kṛṣṇa
kṛṣṇa kṛṣṇa harē harē

NANDALĀLĀ NAVANĪTA

nandalālā navanīta cōra
naṭavara lālā gōpālā

dēvakī vāsudēva kumāra
dēva dēva gōpālā
mōhana murali gāna vilōla
mōhana hari gōpālā

O Son of Nanda, Butter Thief, Dancer and Cowherd Boy, Son of Devaki and Vasudeva, God of gods, Cowherd Boy, Who plays beautiful music on His enchanting flute, O Enchanting Cowherd Boy!

NANDĀ NANDANA HARI

nandā nandana hari
gōvinda gōpāla
ghana śyāma mana mōhanā
gōpi lōlā gōpālā
gōkula bālā gōpālā
hē nanda lālā gōpālā

O Hari, Son of Nanda, Govinda the Cowherd, black like a cloud, Mind-Charmer! The Cowherd Who is soft-hearted towards the Gopis, O Cowherd Boy of Gokula, Son of Nanda!

NANDANA YADU NANDANA

nandana yadu nandana
ānandana citta candana
vandana guru vandana
śrī kṛṣṇa satcidānandana
harē rāma harē rāma
rāma rāma harē harē
harē kṛṣṇa harē kṛṣṇa
kṛṣṇa kṛṣṇa harē harē

O Descendant of Yadu, Delight and Sandal Fragrance of the mind, Reverence to the Guru O Krishna, Existence-Awareness-Bliss.

NĀRĀYAṆA NĀRĀYAṆA JAYA

nārāyaṇa nārāyaṇa jaya govinda harē
nārāyaṇa nārāyaṇa jaya
gōpāla harē

Victory to Narayana, Lord of the cows, Hari! Victory to Naryana, Cowherd Boy, Hari!

NARTANA SUNDARA

nartana sundara natarāja
munijana vandita mahādeva
nartana sundara natarāja

hālā hāladhara
candra kalādhara
gangādhara hara
gauri manōhara
gangādhara gangādhara
hara hara gangādharā

O King of Dancers (Lord Shiva), the Handsome Dancer,O Great God, praised among men and sages, O One Who holds the poison in His throat, Who bears the digit of moon on His forehead, Who bears the Ganga on His head, the Destroyer, Enchanter of Gauri's mind, O Gangadhara Hara!

NATARĀJA NATARĀJA

natarāja natarāja
nartana sundara natarāja
śivarāja śivarāja
śiva kāmi prīya śivarāja
cidambarēśa natarāja
pārvati pate śivarāja

Nataraja, Lord of the Dance, standing before us, Lord Divine. Shivaraja, King Eternal, O Cosmic Dancer, dance the joy of life. O Song of Creation, Nataraja! O Lord of Chidambaram, Lord of Parvati, Shivaraja!

NĀVINTE TUMBIL NIN

nāvinte tumbil nin nāmam tuṭikkumbōl
nerentannariyum ñaṅgaḷ divyamām
nerentannariyum ñaṅgaḷ

O Mother, when Your Name vibrates constantly at the tip of the tongue, we will come to know That which is Real, the Divine.

sukritarāyi tava caraṇa sevakar
ñaṅgaḷ innamme
amṛtānandamayī amme amṛtānandamayī

O Mother Amritanandamayi, today our life finds its consummation in serving Thy Feet.

ñaṅgaḷ mānasa nada turannu
ninnu ātma viśuddhiyōṭe
puṇya kīrtana māla cārtti
indriyangaḷ bhaktiyōṭe

snēha masrina lōlayāyi
lōka sāra pratīkamāyi
uḷḷil vānarulītuka ammē
amṛtānandamayī ammē amṛtānandamayī

O Mother Amritanandamayi, we open the inner sanctum of our heart, and await Thee with attention and inner purity. We have bedecked the inner temple with garlands composed of sacred hymns. Now, please come and abide within the temple, as the Essence of the Universe, as soft and delicate Love.

viśvam pāpa tamassil mungi
martyar svārtha hṛdayarāyi
vittameyta śarangalettu
satya dharmangal oṭungi
śakti ñaṅgaḷ keku nī
andhakāram akattuvān
mukti mārga veḷichamamme
amṛtānandamayī amme amṛtānandamayī

The world is immersed in the darkness of unrighteousness, people have become selfish, and truth and dharma have collapsed under the onslaught of the arrows shot by the relentless pursuit of material wealth. Please give us the strength to eradicate this darkness, O Mother Amritanandamayi, the Beacon on the path to Liberation.

NĪLAMĒGHAṄGAḶE

nīlamēghaṅgaḷe niṅgaḷkkiteṅgane
nēṭān kazhiññinnī nīlavarṇam
vṛndāvanattile nandakumārante
cantameṛum nīla śyāmavarṇam

O blue clouds, how could you gain this azure hue, the charming dark blue complexion of the Child of Nanda at Vrindavan, today?

niṇgaḷ pōyi kanduvō kaṇṇanāmuṇṇiye
taṅgaḷil mindiyō puñcirichō
nīlaravindatten netratāl niṅgaḷe
āpadacūḍam kaṭākṣichuvō

Did you go and meet Kannan Krishna, the child? Did you talk and smile at each other? Did the glance of His eyes, like the blue lotus, caress you from head to toe?

kaṇṇaninnen munnil ettumennōtiyō
enneyum svāgatam ceyyumennōtiyō
en manaśāntikkāyi niṅgaḷ tan kaikaḷil
nalmozhitten tellu tannayachō

Did Kannan tell when He will appear before me? Did He tell that He will welcome me also? Did He send through you a few consoling words for my peace of mind?

NĪLĀÑJANA MIZHI

nīlāñjana mizhi nīrada varṇṇā
nīyē gatiyivanennum, kaṇṇā, kaṇṇā
poyallaviṭunnallā taṭiyanu
illoru śaraṇam kṛṣṇā

Thou art forever my sole refuge, Thou with the complexion of the rain clouds and collyrium-lined blue eyes. It is not a lie, O Krishna, to say that there is none other than Thee to protect me.

bālakumāraka līlakaḷāṭum
śyāmala kōmala kṛṣṇā
nārada tumburu nāda kutūhala
mānasa mōhana kṛṣṇā

O dark and handsome Krishna, playful like a child, who steals the heart and who is attracted by songs of Narada and Tumburu celestial sages.

kīrttana narttana ārttivināśana
sāśvata bhāsura kṛṣṇā
īṣalakannoru vīkṣaṇam ēkuka
sākṣi bhāvābhava [bhāvātmaka] kṛṣṇā

The ever-lustrous Krishna, who dances to devotional songs and Who destroys greed, give me Thy clear vision, Thou who adopts the attitude of a Witness.

māyāmōhana mānavasevita
pādasarōjā kṛṣṇā
bhūtala vāsam akattuka bhagavān
mōkṣa pradāyaka kṛṣṇā

Enchanter of the illusory world, Whose Lotus Feet are being served by men, Bestower of Liberation, please deliver me from this worldly existence, O, Lord Krishna!

NĪ MAṚAN JIRIPPATEṄGU

nī maṛañjirippateṅgu kālikē
sāndramāmī pāri lēkanāyi ñān

Where are You keeping Yourself hidden, Mother Kali? I am alone without You in this world full of Your creatures.

nin viraha vēdanā jvālayil tapippu ñān
ha! poliññiṭunnitā āśa tan pon dīpavum
bhāvamillayō varān pāvamente cāravē
śōkam ēṛiṭunnamme ente hṛttil ākave

I am getting incinerated in the flame of separation from Thee. Alas! Even the golden lamp of hope is getting slowly extinguished. Don't You have any intention of coming to this poor soul? Your absence in the shrine of my heart is leading to increasing pain.

oṭi vannaṇachiṭum amma kezhum kuññine
hanta! nī rasippatō en hṛdayam kezhavē
bhāvamillayō varān pāvamente cāravē
śōkam ēṛiṭunnamme ente hṛttil ākave

A Mother is supposed to come running over and comfort the crying baby. But You, are You just watching the fun while my heart is pining? Don't You have any intention of coming to this poor soul? Your absence in the shrine of my heart is leading to increasing pain.

rāga rōga pīḍayāl ēṛiṭum nirāśayāl
śakti hīnayāyi ñān vīzhvatinnu mumpeyāyi
bhāvamillayō varān pāvamente cāravē
śōkam ēṛiṭunnamme ente hṛttil ākave

Please come before I fall, enfeebled by the disappointments that pile up one after another, as a result of chasing my desires. Don't You have any intention of coming to this poor soul? Your absence in the shrine of my heart is leading to increasing pain.

NIN TIRUPĀDATTIL VĪṆITĀ

nin tirupādattil vīṇitā pāpi
nontakam kezhunnu sādaram
bhītikaḷ pokkiyen mānasam dēva
mōdamanaykkuka daivamē

This sinner has fallen at Thy holy Feet and is crying with an aching heart. Kindly remove my fears and bring joy to my heart, O God.

praṇamichiṭunnu ñān daivamē pāda
tuṇayenikkekuka dēvanē
stūtiyum gītayum allā nī marttya
hṛdayaṅgaḷ nōkkunna nītimān

I bow down to Thee, O God; Thou art not just hymns and songs, but the Lawgiver who looks after human hearts.

kuzhiyil kiṭannu ñān etra nāḷ pāpi
ceḷiyil purandu pōyi etra nāḷ
anuvēlam nin tiru śōṇitam tannu
kanivōṭen ikkoru jīvitam

I lay in the ditch for such a long time. This sinner lay smeared in dirt for such a long time. Manivelan (Lord Subrahmanium) has kindly given me a life.

balahīnayāṇu ñān ezhayil nitya
balavānu daya tōnnuvūzhiyil
irulīḷum ī lōka vazhvilum - tannu
kaniyeṇam tāvakānugraham

I have no strength. The Ever-powerful would have mercy on the helpless. Give me Thy blessing in this darkness, in this earthly life.

ōḷangaḷāl ente jīvita tōṇi
tāzhāte tāṅguka dēvanē
bhaktiyōṭe ninte rūpam smarikkuvān
śakti nalkīṭanam daivamē

Protect the boat of this life from being sunk by the waves. Give me strength to remember Thy Divine Form, O Lord.

NIṚA KĀNTI TIṄGI

niṛa kānti tiṅgi vazhiyum cāru
madhu mandahāsa vadanam
akatāril ennu teḷiyum, annu
bhava rōga śānti viriyum

O Mother, the day Thy effulgent face, adorned with a beatific smile, will fully shine in my inner space, on that day, the disease of worldliness will begin to abate within me.

tirataḷḷiṭunnu vyathakaḷ - ātma
gati kandiṭāte aniśam
iruḷ āzhi āṇu hṛdayam ninnil
teḷiunnatennu jananī

Waves of delusion constantly beat against the inner shores of this mind, and the presence of the Reality within is forever overlooked. This heart is indeed like a dark ocean. When will it see Your Light?

śaraṇāgatarkku taṇalāyi - mevum
vara dāna lōla nayanē
karuṇardra netra munayen hṛttil
patiyān amāntamarutē

O One with eyes of compassion, the Source of solace to those seeking refuge in Thee, I pray that the shafts of compassion emanating from those eyes will swiftly find their mark upon this heart of mine.

kandīṭukente kadanam amba
kandīṭukātma mathanam
uḷḷam tiḷacha kanalil tuḷḷi
veḷḷam taḷikku jananī

O Mother, please see my suffering, this self-inflicted inner torture. Please shower a few drops of cool compassion on these hot embers within.

prānan poriññu bhajanam
ceytu pāram talarnnu jananī
varalunnorente hṛdayam
bhakti rasa dhāra kondu tazhukū

I give my all while singing your hymns, and now I am tired. Please enliven this dried-up heart with the free-flowing nectar of bhakti.

aṛivonnīnālumaṛiyān - ārkkum
arutamba ninte mahimā
aṛiyunna hṛttil amṛtāyi tiṅgi
maruvunnu lōka jananī

O Mother of the Universe, no one can fathom Your greatness with mere intellectual knowledge. You well up like free-flowing ambrosia inside the heart that knows You and You alone.

sampūrṇa puṇya dhanamē - ninne
nambunnu cittamanisam

vembunnamṛtu nuṇayān hṛttil
anpārnudikka jananī

O Divine Wealth, the mind dwells on You at all times, and the heart longs to sip that nectar. Kindly let this heart be Your abode, my Mother.

NIRMALA SNĒHAMĒ

nirmala snēhamē ninne aṟiyātta
jīvitam entinammā
nitya nirāmayī ninne aṟiyātta
jīvitam entinammā

O Pure Love, what is the use of this life without knowing You? Ever blissful one, what is the use of this life, O Mother, without knowing You?

nistula snēhamē ninne aṟiyātta
jīvitam entinammā
mōhana rūpamē ninne ninaykkātta
jīvitam entinammā

O unparalleled Love, without knowing You, O Mother, what is the use of this life? O Mother of attractive form, what is the use of this meaningless life if I am not thinking of You?

mōkṣa sandāyinī ninne labhikkātta
jīvitam dhanyamāṇō
bhaktajana manōhāriṇī ninnuṭe
darśanam ēkukillē

Is this life worthwhile, O Giver of Liberation, without getting You? O Destroyer of the minds of the devotees, won't You give Your darshan?

NITYĀNANDA SATCITĀNANDA

nityānanda satcitānanda
hari hari hari ōm nārāyaṇā
nārāyaṇā hari nārāyaṇā
hari hari hari ōm nārāyaṇā
prēmasvarūpā prēānanda
hari hari hari ōm nārāyaṇā

nityananda	Eternal bliss
satcitānanda	Existence, Awareness, Bliss
hari hari hari	Savior of the afflicted
ōm nārāyaṇa	OM Lord of the primeval waters
prēmasvarûpa	Of the nature of love
prēmānanda	The bliss of love

NṚTTAMĀṬŪ KṚṢṆA

nṛttamāṭū kṛṣṇa naṭanamātū kaṇṇa
venna tarām gōpāla mukunda
venna tarām gōpāla

O Krishna, dance! O Kanna, play! We shall give You butter. O Gopala! O Mukunda!

nṛttam ñān eṅganē ātum sakhikale
dēham taḷarunnu nōvunnu kālukaḷ

How can I dance with my Beloved? My body feels tired and my legs are in pain.

venna tinnēnaham kṣīnam ellām tīrnnu
pātū sakhikale nṛttam ñān vekkunnu

I have eaten the butter and my tiredness is all gone. Come on, my consorts, sing! And I shall dance!

ŌM GURU MĀTĀ

ōm guru mātā sad guru mātā
amṛtānandamayī mama jananī

OM, Mother Who is the Guru, the Perfect Master, my Mother Amritanandamayi.

jaya guru mātā śrī guru mātā
amṛtānandamayī mama jananī

Victory to the Mother Who is the Master, the Auspicious Guru, my Mother Amritanandamayi.

jagad guru mātā param guru mātā
amṛtānandamayī mama jananī

O Mother Who is the Master of the Universe, the Supreme Guru, my Mother Amritanandamayi.

mama guru mātā divya guru mātā
amṛtānandamayī mama jananī

My Guru, Divine Mother, Mother Who is the Guru, my Mother Amritanandamayi.

ŌM KĀLI ŌM MĀTĀ

ōm kāli ōm mātā
durga tē namō namā
śakti kuṇḍalīnī jagad kē mātā

Om Kali, Om Mother, salutations to Durga, to the Kundalini Shakti, the Mother of the World.

ŌMKĀRA DIVYA PORŪḶE VI

ōmkāra divya porūḷe varū
ōmana makkaḷe vēgam
ōmanayāyi valarnāmayangal nīkki
ōmkāra vastu āyi tīrū

Come quickly darling children; you are the Essence of Om. Removing all sorrows, grow as endearing ones and become one with the sacred syllable OM.

snēhattāl lōkam jayīkkū makkaḷ
jñānārkka tejassutīrkū
dhyānonmukham bhakti bhāvōjvalam snēha
sāndram hṛdantam pulartū

Win the world over by love, children, and keep your hearts turned to meditation, glowing with devotion and suffused with love.

deśa samskāram vetinyāl pinne
seṣippatentānu nammiḷ
lōkattinītutta sandēśamekuvān
ī manninuntinnu mennum

If we discard the cultural heritage of our land, what else remains in us? This land always has an enduring message to give to the world.

ārōtum uḷḷinte uḷḷil makkaḷ
snēhādārangal pularttū
āreyum ullariñādarikunnavar
ādara vazhiykkum mannil

Children, keep love and respect for everyone alive in you. One who gives heartfelt respect to all will deserve respect on this world.

lōka samādhāna dautyam
janma sāphalyam ennōrtunarū
vyakti vairaṅgalum svārtha mōhaṅgalum
citta daurbalya mānorkkū

Children, be awake with the thought that the mission of peace in the world means life's fulfillment. Remember that personal rivalries and selfish desires indicate weakness of the mind and heart.

ōlamattāzha katal pōl manam
ekānta śānta māyi tīrān
jīvitāsleshikal ākunna cintakal
ekikarīkkuken makkaḷ

To make your mind one-pointed and still as the waveless ocean, my children, all your thoughts should be brought to a focus in the Self.

dāsōha bhāvam pulartū makkaḷ
svāsthyam manassinnunarttū
vākkil rasam vēṇam vēṇam dayārdratā
vēṇam svadharmāvabōdham

Children, nurture the attitude that "I am a servant." Nurture firmness of mind. Be charming in your words, be melting with compassion and be aware of your duty (dharma).

kaivalya dhāmam teḷikkām amma
kai piṭichhennum nayīykkam
kaitavam vēnta samādhāna cittarāyi
ceyyūkakartavya karmam

Amma will clear the path to Liberation. She will hold your hand and lead you to the goal. Be truthful and carry out your life's responsibilities, and in this way you will attain peace of mind.

vyakti svātantryatte makkaḷ verum
tucha kāryārthamākkāte
martya lōkattin vimuktikkuṭātamām
kṛtyangalāl dhanyamākkū

Children, do not waste your personal freedom in pursuit of inconsequential things. Enrich your freedom through noble deeds aimed at the freedom of all mankind.

vidvēṣa buddhiyil makkaḷ svayam
niṣpati cīdā tirikkū
tyāga sannadharāyi svārtha vihīnarāyi
jīvitānandam pakarū

Do not fall into spitefulness, my children. Spread the joy of life through renunciation and selflessness.

uṇṇata yādhārdhya bōdham uḷḷil
uṇṇidra mākatte yennum
uḷḷatil nanmayum uṇṇatādarśavum
uḷḷavarkillalil eṅgum

Let the awareness of the Supreme Reality be always alive in you. Those who have truth and high ideals at heart will be free from suffering.

tulyarānammakku makkaḷ ennāl
tellum sahikkilla dharmam
kṛṣṇan sahichilla rāman sahichilla
ārum sahikilladharmam

All Her children are equal in Mother's eyes. But Mother cannot tolerate even a bit of evil (adharma). Krishna did not tolerate evil, nor did Rama. No one will put up with it.

jātiyāl nīcarallārum nīca
karmattāl nīcarākunnū
ātma samskāram
telinyor savarnarān allel avar

No one is low by birth (caste). Lowly conduct makes people low. Those who make their hearts shine through refinement are high caste; others are low.

āśrayikkunnavar kīsan hrittil
svāsraya bōdham teḷikkyum
āsrita vatsalan ārti vināśanan
kleśa karmaṅgal haniykkum

God will develop the sense of self-reliance in those seeking His refuge. He to Whom refuge seekers are beloved, Who destroys grief, He will destroy all afflictions.

ceyyunna karmatinotta phalam
koyentavar nammalellām
ceyyāte ceyyunna karmaṅgal tan phalam
koyyāte koyyentatum nām

We will reap the fruit of what we sow. For unthinking, impulsive actions, fitting results will come on their own.

kāma karmaṅgal tyajiykkū makkaḷ
jñāna karmōlsukha rākū
vēda śāstratin velichetāl samsāra
śōkandhakāram akattū

Children, give up actions driven by desires. Turn your interest to actions guided by knowledge (of the scriptures). With the light of Vedic teachings, drive away the darkness of the grief caused by worldly attachments.

munnil viḷikkunnu daivam māya
pinnil talakkunnu namme
māyā mayārnavam nīntikadakkuvān
māyanam dehātma bhāvam

God calls us to go forward; Maya (illusion) pulls us backward. To swim across the great ocean of Maya, one has to lose awareness of the body and the small self.

vidhramippikkyunnu māyā svantam
viśva rachana yilūte satya mallengīlum
satyamāyi tonnikkyum
rajjuvil sarpam kanakke

Maya bewilders us through the act of creating this universe. Untruth appears to be truth as a rope appears to be a snake.

māyakkarutāttatillā makkaḷ
māyā vipatil petolle māya kadīnarāyi
mazhkāthe mānasam
mōhavimuktamākkīdu

Nothing is impossible for Maya, children. Don't fall into the calamity called Maya. Don't become victims of illusion and lament; free your mind from its clutches.

samsāra bījam naśichāl svayam
santāpa nāśam bhavikkyum
antarangattinna gādhatayil mulla
kumbum ahantayām bījam

When the seed of samsara (the cycle of birth and death), the seed of egotism that sprouts in the deepest depths of the mind, is dead, then sorrows end of themselves.

paurūsham nedinām namme
divya bhāvattile kuyar tenam
vyakti satvam paripūrṇamāyi daivattil
arppichu pūrṇarākēṇam

Having attained human form, we should elevate ourselves to the Divine. We should surrender our individual selves totally to God and thus become perfect.

veṣa vidhānattinallā
mano bhāvattinānu prādhānyam
ārbhāta bhaktiyum ārava pūravum
ātma lakṣyam telikkillā

The state of your clothes is not important, but the state of your mind is. Devotion to grandeur and show will not illuminate one toward the goal of the Self.

ātanka harṣangal onnum
ātma dharma mallōrkkuvin makkaḷ
ārumuyarttu killātmāvine svayam
ātma varinyunar tenam

Children, sorrows and joys are not attributes of the Self. No one else will elevate the self; the self will have to elevate itself.

dehōham yennōrtirunnāl
bhōga jālatil āśa vardhikum
bhōgā śayil ninnum krōdham jvalichīdum
krodhāgni ulkām berikkum

If you live thinking, "I am this body," then desire for the myriad sensory pleasures will increase. From such desires anger arises and the flames of anger will burn the tender shoots within.

uḷḷam malarke turakkū makkaḷ
ulvili kēḷkkān śramikkū
tannullilāzhattil verunni nilkku mā
janma samskāra mazhikkū

Children, open your heart wide. Try to hear the call within. Untie those bonds of training begun at birth, which are rooted deep within you.

ekamānīśvara premam
nānā devatā bhāvangal pōnam
varnōjvalā kāra bhāvangal okkeyum
eka sārattilākkeṇam

Love of God is one-pointed. One should be free of the concept of different deities. All the colorful resplendent forms should merge in the Essential One.

ārilum lōkaika nāthan snēha
tūmaram tam tūki nilpū
ānavum pōkukil āmaya nāśanan
āreyum vārippunarum

The Supreme Lord of the Universe showers the nectar of love on everyone. When the smallness of our heart fades, He, the Destroyer of sorrow, will lift us up and embrace us.

canchalam nīngum tapassil śakti
sambhari cītuvin makkal
uḷḷile śaktiyil ulsāha cittarāyi
uddīpta mākkuvin lōkam

Children, build up your strength through penance which removes unsteadiness. With joyous hearts, make the world glow with your inner strength.

unnata sthānangal onnum namme
unnata rākkilla tōrkū
ātmāvinaunnatyam
ārān jariñjavar ātmāvilunnatam nedum

Remember that none of the high positions in the world uplift us. One who seeks for and knows the heights within oneself will become uplifted.

śriṣtiyil dūṣya millottum kānum
drishtitan dūshya mānellām
driṣti dōsham kondu śriṣti dūshyam varum
driṣti mānyal śriṣti māyum

Creation is faultless. All the faults lie in the eyes of the viewer. Faulty vision will bring fault to the Creation. If the eyes become dim, so will the Creation.

varnanā vaibhavam venam hṛttil
mangātanubhūti vēṇam
nānā viṣayatil vēṇam parijñānam
vēṇam prapañcāva bōdham

Children, one should have the power of expression and have compassion. One should acquire knowledge of diverse subjects and a deep perception of the universe.

mantra svarūpam manassil
sadā mangāthe vartikkumenkil
mandī bhavikkilla mānasam
santāpa cintakal mañastamīkkum

If the form of the Chosen Deity always stays shining in the mind, then the mind will never weaken and sorrowful thoughts will fade and disappear.

mekhathāl mūdunna sūryan
vīndum sōbhichhu minnunna pōle
ajñāna ghōrāndha kāram poliyukil
hṛttil vīlangum svarūpam

Just as the sun, once covered by clouds, re-emerges and shines again, so will the Self shine within when the terrible darkness of ignorance lifts.

pinnōttu pōkilla kālam makkaḷ
munnōttati vechu pōkū
vankārya sādhyatte munnirtti
jīvitam munnōttu sukṣmam nayīkkū

Time never moves backwards, children. Go forward step by step keeping the Supreme Aim in view. Guide your life forward carefully.

dānavan vānavanākām vīndum
vānavan dānavanākām
vānava dānava mānava samskāram
mānava hṛttilundōrkkū

Someone demonic can turn into someone divine and vice versa. Remember: the good and evil qualities of man, god and demon, are in the human heart.

tatvārtha buddhiyil makkaḷ
sadā nisvārtha jīvitam nedū
vyakti bōdhatin nahanta
yattul kalam arppikka daivattil makkaḷ

Children, always lead a selfless life and seek the higher truths. Control your egocentric nature and surrender your heart to God.

uḷḷam telīvuttu narnāl tante
uḷḷum puravum kulirkkum
audārya sīlavum anyōnya
maitriyum uḷḷinnura vāyītenam

When your heart clears and awakens, the inner and outer lives become joyful. Generosity and friendship for each other arise from the fountain within you.

tān tanikkenna vichāram nīngi
nām namukkenākum eppōl
svargam svayam tānīrangum dharītriye
kalpaka pūvādiyākkum

When the thought "I, for me," changes into "we, for us," then heaven will by itself come down to earth. This is like the flower of the wish-fulfilling tree, the fulfillment of all desires.

mantra japā vartanattāl
citta vrittikalellām atangi
niṣhpanda mākukil
satyā vabodhattin
nistulānandam nirayum

When the mind becomes still, and all mental activity is stopped through repetition of a mantra, then the unequalled bliss of knowledge of the Truth will fill us inside.

OMKĀRA DIVYA PORŪḶE VII

ōmkāra divya porūḷe varu
ōmana makkaḷe vēgam
ōmanayāyi valar nāmayaṅgal nīkki
ōmkāra vastuvāyi tiru

Come quickly darling children, you who are the divine essence of OM. Remove all sorrows, grow to be adorable and merge with the sacred OM.

uḷḷilundānanda sāram uḷḷil
cellāykil illennu tonnum
ellilunnenna nam kaṇāykayālatum
illāte āvilla nūnam

The essence of bliss is ever present in our inner most core, but its reality cannot be experienced if we do not enter there. The existence of oil within the sesame seed cannot be denied even though it is not visible outside of the seed.

makkaḷkku nervazhi nalkān amma
vyagrathayōdadukkunnu
sikṣanam venam suniscitha lakṣyati
nakṣina yatnam pradhānam

Mother is eagerly guiding the children in the right path. In order to reach the goal, guidance, teachings and tireless effort are important.

sammiśramāninnu hṛttil bahu
janmārjitam karma bījam
bhinna samskārangal tingiyadaññuḷḷi
lengum tirakkol uyartum

The seed of karma in each of us is a mixture of vasanas (tendencies) acquired through several past lives. The pressure of such varied vasanas will create turbulence inside us.

uḷḷile caitanya dhārā namme
nāmākki nirtunnu nityam
mānava dharmam marannātha ātmāvil
onnum aham buddhi tāne

The ever present divine flow inside us moulds us into what we are. Once we forget the real nature of a human being, only the ego remains.

svāsattil sōham japippu vīndum
dēham tānennortirippu
ulvili kēḷkkān aṟiyāykayālanya
dharmam svadharma mennennum

The chant of SOHAM (I am He) is repeated through every breath, yet we think we are the body. Due to ignorance of recognizing this inner chant, our own actions are wrongly considered as the divine Dharma.

kleśangalentum sahichum hṛttil
īśvara prēmam nirakkyu
kleśam cilappōl cilarkk ātmadhairyattin
ākkamekām makkaḷorkkū

We should fill our hearts with divine love even if it requires much suffering. Children, remember that suffering often builds up our self-confidence.

bhāvartha mulkkondu makkaḷ bhakti
gānāmritam nukarnnīdu
tatvam grahikyākil bhakti urakkilla
bhaktiyilel illa mukti

Enjoy the nectar of divine songs appreciating their inner meaning. Bhakti (devotion) cannot take root in our mind without knowing the Truth. There is no mukti (Liberation) without bhakti.

nirvachikyāva tallārkkum neril
nirmala bhakti svarūpam
bhaktiyum muktiyum
randalla svātmāvil sraddha tangum bhakti yuktam

The nature of pure devotion cannot be defined precisely by anyone. Bhakti and mukti are not two separate entities. Bhakti coupled with faith in our own soul is most appropriate.

bhōgasamskāram vedingu makkaḷ
tyāga samskāram valartu
lōka śāntikkyāyi svāyam
samarppichu nām snēha sandēśam parattu

Children, renounce the craving for worldly pleasures and cultivate the habit of selfless service. Dedicate yourself to the cause of world peace and spread the message of love.

lōlamāvenum manassu dhairyam
corāte sūkshi citeṇam
anya dukhangalil maññupōl mānasam
nannāyi aliñño zhukeṇam

The mind has to be soft and tender, but at the same time, be vigilant not to lose courage. Seeing the suffering of others, our mind should melt like snow.

uḷḷāl mahatvam grahichāl ārum
nallavar ānennu kāṇān
ulveḷichem vēṇam ellārilum tangum
divyata neril darśikkyān

If we recognize the greatness of our inner real nature, we will see only goodness in everyone. Only with our own inner divine light can we witness the divine light present in others.

munnil undamma eppozhum pāta
nannāyi telikkyān nayikkyān
makkaḷ tīriññu nilkkumbozhānammaye
hṛttil darśikkyāta torku!

Mother is always leading and guiding the children showing the right path, but remember that when the children face backwards they will be unable to see Mother in their hearts.

nintā stuthikalil onnum manam
tangātilakkam varāte
svastharāyi susthira
vastuvil nityavum cittatārarpikka makkaḷ

Children, do not get perturbed by praise or insult. Maintain calm composure and concentrate only on the Eternal Being.

nirmala snēhardra cittam namme
viśva jetākkalakkunnu
ādarśa saurabham mattum manasullor
ārogya pūrṇarāvunnu

We can win the entire world with pure loving hearts. When the mind is filled with the aroma of noble thoughts, one is strong and healthy.

mōhana svapnangal mātram kondu
jīvitam neyyarutārum
pinpottu nōkkuvin tellida pinneyum
munpottu pōkuvin makkaḷ

Don't weave your lives only out of beautiful dreams. Children, look back for a short while and then proceed.

kūrtu mūrtastram kanakke lakṣyam
bhedichidum satva buddhi
satyam svayam hṛdi
vyaktamāvān karma śuddhi vēṇam jīvitattil

Like a sharp pointed arrow, the pure intellect will hit and pierce the goal. Purity of action is needed in one's life in order to experience the real nature of the Self.

kāttatulayunna dīpam etu
nerathum tāne anayām
dehatil tangunnorāyussum vegatil
tāne poliññu poyidām

The flame flickering in the wind can get extinguished at any time. Similarly the life in the body can flow out of it at any moment.

kālam kanakkattu namme mannil
vāzhikkayillennatōrtāl
vīndum janichum marichum mahattāya
marttya janmam tulakkyāmo?

If we are aware of the fact that time will make no error in deciding our life span on this planet, can we still afford to waste this great human life and continue again on the cycle of birth and death?

mānatte mārivil pōle māyum
mōhana saubhāgya jālam
jīvita sārārtha pāthayariññu nām
pōkukil janma sāphalyam

Life will be enriched if we continue on the path leading to the real purpose of life. The illusion of pleasure will disappear like a rainbow in the sky.

mānavaikyat tinde mantram makkaḷ
mārāte hṛttil smarikkû
lōkam samādari cīdunnu nammuṭe
jīvāvabōdha mahatvam

Children, always remember in your heart the mantra of the unity of all human beings. The entire world respects the greatness of human consciousness.

kāpatya millātta neñjam śobha
terunna svarlōka tulyam
niṣkala bhāvarka cettassil tingunna
satyānubhūti ennennum

The glow of a pure innocent heart is equal to heaven. The experience of the Truth is embedded permanently in the glow of the sun of innocence.

vēṇam gurutvam manassil sadā
vēṇam guruvil viśvāsam
īśvaran munnil guruvāyi varum namu
kīśanil vāzhvanachidān

The Grace of Guru is essential; one should always have faith in Guru. God will appear before us as our Guru to receive our life as an offering.

sandeha millorutellum tulya
snēhame ammekkariyu
ādhyātma vidyayil
śraddhayullor snēham
ammāyilerayayi kānmū

There is no doubt that Mother knows only how to love all equally without any bias. Yet only spiritual aspirants will experience that love in abundance.

nūṟu nūṟāgrahakketil venu
nerunñu marthya hṛdantam
nediyatellām nirartha mennākilum
neduvānerinnu mōham

The human heart entangled with hundreds of desires burns with sorrow and pain. Even though knowing fully well that all those desires which were fulfilled did not bring any happiness, we still pursue them foolishly.

veṇal mazha pōle vēgam varum
pōkum sukha dukha bhāvam
randum tudarnnu nilkkilla varandinnum
mīte mānassurya tenam

Pleasure and pain will come and go as summer showers. Both are short lived. We should lift our minds above those two.

rōgāturam tanne cittam lakṣya
bōdham talirkkāthirunnāl
mayāprapañchatilarkkum aham buddhi
mārāttha vyādhiyā norkku

The human mind is stricken with disease if it is not vibrant with the thoughts of a goal-oriented life. Remember that the egoistic mind is an untreatable disease having its roots in the illusory world.

ennum ñān nin kālkkalallo svanta
bandhuvum nī mātramallo
innu nī yenne vediññā lulakil
pinnennum ñān ālambahīnan

I am always near Your lotus feet. I have no other relations except You. If You desert me today, I will always be an orphan.

yennīvīdham manōbhāvam sadā
tingum manassiludīkkyum
ammayum kāṇum prapañca caitanyavum
bhinna mallannenna bōdham

If the mind is filled with such thoughts (see the previous verse), the awareness of oneness with Mother, the Divine Essence behind the universe, will shine in the mind.

tannil ninnanyamāyi tonnum lōkam
tan manōbhāva pratīkam
ñānennum nīyennum uḷḷa bhedam bhuvi
māyā vimōha mennorkku

The world appears separate from us because of our mental projections. Remember that the feeling of distinction between you and I is only due to Maya (illusion).

mandāra puṣpa samānam hṛttil
mangala cinta vidarthi
cāru saundaryavum pūvamṛtam pāri
lāke ozhukkuken makkaḷ

Let noble thoughts blossom like flowers in our mind. Children, let the honey and beauty from such flowers flow into the world unhindered.

cintakaḷkkellām orantyam svantam
antarangattil nām kānkil
ellām orātmāvennullā lariññu nām
tallāte uḷkkollumellām

All thoughts come to an end if we realize that everything is but the One.

ārādhana manōbhāvam vēṇam
ācarikkunnattil ellām
ārava pūravum arbhāda bhaktiyum
ātma lakṣyatte marakkyam

Whatever we do should be done as worship. Festivities and enjoyments associated with worldly extroverted devotion will hide the goal of Self-realization.

kūttāyi pravartikka makkaḷl lōka
kūttāyi mayil viśvasikku
kūttāya soddeśa karmangalāl viśva
mottāke aiśvaryam muttam

Work as a team, chidren. Believe in the united spirit of the world. Noble actions performed unitedly will easily bring prosperity to the world.

onnānu nammaḷ ennothum marttyar
pinneyum bhinnichu mārum
ekata yātma svabhāva mānalātte
deha svabhāvamallorkku

We say we are united, but people live divided and act incohesively. Remember that unity is the inherent character of the soul and not of the physical bodies.

bhaktiyum śraddhayum vēṇam yukti
bhadrata yetilum vēṇam
hṛttil nirantaram bhakti yurakkyukil
mukti pinnentinnu vere

One should have faith and devotion. If one has constant devotion rooted in the heart, what is the need for Mukti?

lōkam pazhikkyām chīlappōl namme
neru darśikkyāthirikkyām
kālam telikkyum kṣamikka
nam nanmakaḷ tālōlichullil valarttu

Sometimes the world may not appear to be all right. We may not see the Truth; but be patient. Times will change for the better. Cultivate good thoughts in the mind.

teṭunnu svātantryam engum marttyan
vīzhunnu vīndum vipathil
svātantryam ātmāvilānenna torāte
jīvitam ārāsvadikkum?

Man seeks for liberation but again and again falls back into sorrow and suffering. Who can enjoy life without recogizing that real freedom lies deep in the soul?

saccharitangal sravikku hṛittil
sadvichārangal nirakku
satya dharmattil carikkyu nirantaram
sachil svarūpam smarikku

Listen to good noble stories; fill the mind with illuminating thoughts. Practice honesty and Dharma. Meditate on a divine form always.

lōka śāntikkyāyi nammaḷ ennum
jīvichu pōnnavarallo
lōkā samasta sukhīnō bhavantu
vennā mantra morkuken makkaḷ

We have been living for a long time dedicated to world peace. Children, remember the mantra "Lokah samastah sukhino bhavantu" (May the whole world be happy).

ŌMKĀR GURU MĀ ŌMKĀR

ōmkār guru mā ōmkār
ōmkār guru mā ōmkār
ōmkār guru mā ōmkār

The syllable OM is itself the beloved Guru-Mother and the beloved Guru-Mother is the very essence of OM

ŌM NAMŌ BHAGAVATE VĀSUDĒVĀYA

ōm namō bhagavate vāsudēvāya
ōm namō bhagavate vāsudēvāya
ōm nama śivāya
ōm namō nārāyaṇāya

Om! Salutations to the Lord in Whom all exists. Salutations to the Auspicious One (Shiva)! Salutations to the Lord Who rests on the Waters!

ŌM ŚRĪ MĀTĀ JAGANMĀTĀ

ōm śrī mātā jaganmātā
vandē mātā jaganmātā

O Mother, Mother of the universe in the form of the sacred syllable OM, I pray to You. O Mother of the universe, please save me.

līla vigraha dhāriṇī
lalanā rūpa vihāriṇī
jayatu sadā bhavatāriṇī
lasatu sadā hṛdi hāriṇī

You are appearing in a human form as a mere sport. You play in a supple and elegant form. May You Who take us across the ocean of mundane existence, be ever victorious. O pure auspicious One who captivates my heart.

śūla kapāla vinōdinī
śaradamalendu suhāsinī
śritajana mānasa hamsinī
śamaya vyadhām bhava bhañjinī

You sport with the trident and skull. Your smile is as cool as the faultless moon. You are the swan in the Manasa lake of the beings that take refuge in You. Please cure our ills, O Devi, Who can break the cycle of births and deaths.

anupama karuṇā śālini
akhila janāmaya śūlini
subhada sukhāmṛta mālini
kalayatu mē hṛdi pāvani

Your kindness has no comparison. You destroy the troubles of those who seek refuge in You with Your trident. You dispense the auspicious nectar of bliss. O pure One, please be present in my heart always.

ORU NĀḶUM PIRIYĀTTO

oru nāḷum piriyātto - rōrmayumāyi
tirayāttiṭam viraḷam ammē
ulakīrezhil umayāḷe tēṭi ñān
alayāttidam viraḷam pala janmam
alayāttiṭam viraḷam

Mother, the places where I have not searched for You, keeping You incessantly in my mind, are rare. The worlds in which I have not roamed about, in the course of many a life-time searching for my Uma (the consort of Shiva, the Mother of the Universe) are but few.

vilakeṭṭa jīvitamāyi tīrnnuvō -ente
vijaya pratīkṣa tan piṭi viṭṭuvō
pakaliravorupōle paravaśanāyi ñān
pādayātra ceyunnitā lakṣya
veḷiviṅgal tala cāykkuvān
ammē, ammē, ammē, ammē

Has this also become a worthless life? Have I lost my grip on the expected final victory? I am nevertheless continuing this journey, frustrated though I am, neither stopping by day or night until I can rest my head with the Goal in sight.

phaṇamuyarttunnuvō pinneyum durmadam
gati nirōdhikkayō durvidhi pinneyum
varanduṇaṅgumen hṛdaya vanikayil
amṛta mazha coriyū ammē
akatāril kuḷirēku nī
ammē, ammē, ammē, ammē

Are my negative tendencies once again rearing their head like a cobra raising its hood? Is my unfavourable destiny once again blocking the way? Please shower Your nectarous Grace on the dry river bed of my heart. Mother, please make that cool stream flow again.

PĀṆḌURANGA VIṬHALĀ

pāṇḍuranga viṭhalā hari hari viṭhalā
nārāyaṇa viṭhalā hari hari viṭhalā
rādhē śyāma viṭhalā hari hari viṭhalā
nandalālā viṭhalā hari hari viṭhalā

paṇḍuranga	Of white color
viṭhalā	Lord Vishnu
hari	Savior of the distressed
nārāyaṇa	Lord of the primeval waters
rādhē śyāma	Radha and Krishna
nandalala	Son of Nanda

PARAVAŚAMĀṆEN HṚDAYAM

paravaśamāṇen hṛdayam jananī
bahuvidha cintākulamāyi
arutarutiniyum viḷamba marute
agatiye akatār karutān ī
agatiye akatār karutān

Mother, my mind is much distressed with so many distracting thoughts. Don't delay anymore to pay attention to this destitute!

alakaṭal naṭuvil agādhatayil
aśaraṇan ñānenaṛiyū!
aśrulaya mizhikaḷ kāśrayamaruḷān
viśruta caritē varumō? (3x)

Know that I am helplessly falling into the deep sea! O Mother of well-known history, won't You come to give solace to my weeping eyes?

bahuvidha durita tirakaḷuyarnen
hṛdayam nibaddhitammallō [prachalitamallō]
piṭayukayāṇī agni samudrē
maṛukara kāṇātiniyum nin
padamalar kāṇātiniyum

Isn't my mind confused with so many unfortunate waves? I am writhing in this oceanic fire without reaching the shore, without seeing Your lotus feet yet.

PARAYŪ SAKHI MAMA

parayū sakhi mama hṛdayādhināyakan
karimukiloli varṇṇaneṅgu pōyi?
hṛdayam takarunnu nayanam
nanayunnu
vazhikānātatitetti vīnitunnu

My dear friend, tell me where has the Lord of my heart, that dark-complexioned one, gone? My heart is breaking, my eyes are wet, I am falling, not seeing the path.

piṭayunna jīvane tatayānum vayyahō
parayū sakhi kaṇṇaneviṭeyāmō
kṣana nēram vayyini piriyānen nāthane
karaḷ nīri nīriyente antyamāyi

Alas, I can't control the writhing life force! Dear friend, tell me where is Krishna? Oh, I can't bear the separation from my Lord anymore. I am going to die due to the ceaseless burning of my heart.

oru tettum ceyyāttorī rādhayiṅgane
karayu vānitayāyatentu tozhi kaṇṇā
ā krūran kondupōyi madhuraykku kaṇṇane
akrūranennoru peru nalki

Friend, why is this faultless Radha ordained to weep like this? Who has given the cruel man (Kruran) who took Kanna to Mathura, the name "not cruel" (Akruran)?

kaṇṇan pirannorā madhurāpuriykkahō
śāpam kotukuvān vaya tōzhī kaṇṇa
kaṇṇante bhaktanāna krūranum sakhī
ellāmī rādha tan kāla dōṣam

Friend, I can't curse that holy city Mathura, where Kanna took His birth! That "not cruel" one is also a devotee of Kanna, my friend; everything is due to this Radha's bad times.

karayalle priyasakhi ñān maricchītukil
parayane nī pōyi kaṇṇanōtu
"karunānidhe ninte priyadāsi rādhika
virahattī pitipeṭṭu ventu pōyi!"

My dear friend, don't cry! If I die, you must go to Kanna and tell Him, "O Compassionate One, Your beloved servant Radhika was burnt in the fire of separation."

oru vidham taṅgippitichenne śyāmante
arikilettikumō vallapātum
śakti ente maranattil karayano vidhinin
iniyente kaṇṇane kāṇumō ñān

Somehow supporting me, can you take me near that dark-complexioned one? My companion, is it your fate to weep over my death? Will I ever see my Kanna?

vṛndāvana lōla rādha priyankara
nin rādha prāṇanvetinnitate
en cita bhasmattilittiri nī ninte
netiyil puśumō prēmamurtte

O the delicacy of Vrindavana, Radha's sweetheart! Let Your Radha leave her body! O Love Incarnate, will You smear Your forehead with the ashes from my cremation?

PĀVANA GANGĒ TĀYĒ

pāvana gangē tāyē pāpa nāśinī nī
ardhanārīśante śirassil vasiykkum
pīyūṣagāyikē*

O sacred Ganga, Mother, Thou art the Destroyer of sins. Thou dwellest upon the head (matted hair knot) of Shiva, who has Parvati as the left half of His body, O Singer whose voice flows like nectar.

gangē śaṅkarajaṭā vāsinī
gangē himālayavāsini
māyā vimōcini kaluṣa vināśinī
śiva hṛnmōhini jagadambikē
mōha vināśinī pāpa vimōcini
vidyādāyinī mātā gangē

O Ganga, who resides in Shiva's hairknot, O Ganga, who resides in the Himalayan Mountains, O Universal Mother, Thou art the remover of the cosmic delusion, the destroyer of sins and the beloved of Shiva.

vēdasvarūpiṇī gangē
ānandarūpiṇi gangē
jai bhayahāriṇī jai bhavatārinī

duṣcintāhāriṇī jagadambikē
mōhavināśinī

O Ganges, the embodiment of the Vedas, the embodiment of bliss. Hail to Thee, destroyer of fear. Hail, Mother, who helps one cross the ocean of transmigration, destroyer of evil thoughts, O Universal Mother.

bhāgīrathī śivamanōharī
bhāgīrathī kṛpā sāgarī
sarvajanēśvarī dēvī śaṅkarī,
dēvī bhagavatī jagadambikē
mōhavināśini

O Bhagirathi (daughter of Bhagiratha), beloved of Shiva, ocean of kindness. O Universal Mother, Devi Bhagavathi, Thou art the ruler of mankind, the Goddess who brings auspiciousness.

PRABHŌ GAṆAPATĒ

prabhō gaṇapatē paripūraṇa vāzh varuḷ vāyē
śārntu vaṇaṅki stuti pāṭiyāṭi untan
sannidhi śaraṇa mataintōmē
śānta citta saubhāgyam yāvayum
tantaruḷ sadguru nīyē

O Lord Ganapati, Giver of perfect life, dancing and singing we will surrender at Your feet, O Sadguru, Giver of peaceful minds and all fortunes.

ādi mûla gaṇanātha gajānana
atbhutadhvaḷa svarūpā
dēva dēva jaya vijaya vināyaka
cinmaya paraśivadīpā

ādi mûla	The root cause
Gaṇanatha	The leader of Shiva's army
Gajānana	Elephantfaced atbhuta dhavala
svarûpa	The one with a wonderful white form
dēvadēva	The Lord of all gods
jayavijaya	Victorious
vināyaka	Remover of all obstacles
cinmaya	Supreme Truth
paraśivadīpā	The Light of auspiciousness

tēṭi tēṭi eṅkō ōṭukinrār - unnai
tēṭi kandu koḷḷalāmē
kōṭi kōṭi madayānaikaḷ paṇiceyyum
kunṟena viḷaṅkum pemmānē

People run searching for You but they can find You if they search inside. You, who are served by tens of millions of strong elephants, have numerous capabilities.

jñāna vairāgya vicāra sāra svara
rāgalaya naṭanapādā
nāma bhajana guṇa kīrttana vividha
nāyaka jaya jagannāthā

You are the Essence of knowledge, dispassion, and contemplation. You dance rhythmically to the different notes. O Lord of the Universe, victory unto You! O Leader, the many kinds of chants, bhajans and glorifications are done for Your sake.

pārvati bāla apāra parāpara
parama bhāgavata bhavatāraṇa
bhaktajana sumukha praṇava vināyaka
pāvana parimaḷa caraṇā

pārvatibala	The son of Goddess Parvati
apāra parāpara	Transcendent
paramabhāgavata	Foremost among devotees
bhavatārana	The boatman who helps one to cross over the ocean of transmigration
bhaktajana-samukha	Giver of happiness to devotees
prāṇava	Omkara
vināyaka	Remover of all obstacles
pāvana	Purifier
parimaḷacaraṇā	One whose feet smell nicely

PRABHUJI TUM CHANDAN

prabhuji tum chandan ham pāni
jāke ang ang mās samāye
prabhuji tum chandan ham pāni

O Lord, You are sandalwood and I am water. When we are together there is a divine fragrance.

prabhuji tum ghan ban ham mōra
jaise chitvat chandra chakōra
prabhuji tum khanban ham mōra

O Lord, You are dense clouds and I am like a peacock in a jungle. You are like the glow of the full moon and I am like a chakora bird (that feeds on moonbeams).

prabhuji tum dīpak ham bāti
jāki jōt bharai din rāti
prabhuji tum dīpak ham bāti

O Lord, You are the lamp and I am a wick from which light will shine day and night.

prabhuji tum mōti ham dhāgā
jese sōlah milite suhāgā
prabhuji tum mōti ham dhāgā

O Lord, You are the pearl and I am the thread. We together will make a beautiful rosary.

prabhuji tum svāmi ham dāsā
aisi bhakti karai rō dāsā
prabhuji tum svāmi ham dāsā

O Lord, You are my Master. Poet Raidas wants to serve You as Your devoted servant.

RĀDHĒ GŌVINDA BHAJŌ

rādhē gōvinda bhajō rādhē gōvinda
rādhā ramaṇa hari rādhē gōvinda
rādhē rādhē rādhē rādhē rādhē gōvinda

rādhē	Beloved of Krishna
gōvinda	Lord of the cows
bhajō	Worship
ramaṇa	Beautiful One
hari	Who relieves distress

RĀDHĒ RĀDHĒ RĀDHĒ ŚYĀM

rādhē rādhē rādhē śyām
rādhā mādhava śyām
prēma śyām sundara śyām
rādhē rādhē rādhē śyām

gōpī mōhana kṛṣṇa
śyām rādhē kṛṣṇa

gōkula vāsi kuñjavihāri
rādha mādhava kṛṣṇa

kṛṣṇa kṛṣṇa rādhākṛṣṇa
muralī mōhana kṛṣṇa (4x)

gōvardhana giridhāri
vṛndāvana sañcāri
nanda kumārā navanīta cōrā
manasija mōhana kṛṣṇa
kṛṣṇa kṛṣṇa rādkṛṣṇa (4x)

gōkula vāsi	One who lives in Gokul
gōpimōhan	One who enchants the cowherd girls
gōvardhana giri-dhari	One who supported the Govardhana hill
kuñjavihari	One who sports in the groves
manasija mōhana	One who attracts our minds
prēma	Loving one
sundar	Beautiful
śyām	One who is dark-complexioned
vṛndāvanasañcāri	One who walks in Vrindavan

RĀDHĒ RĀDHĒ ŚYĀMA

rādhē rādhē śyāma rādhē
rādhē rādhē śyām
rādhē śyām rādhē śyām
rādhē śyām rādhē śyām
rādhē rādhē rādhē rādhē

rādhē	Beloved of Krishna
śyām	Dark colored (Krishna)

RĀDHIKĀ MANŌHARĀ

rādhikā manōharā
madana gōpālā
dīnavatsalā hē bālagōpālā
bhaktajana mandāra vēṇugōpālā

muralidhara hē gānavilōlā
harē rāma harē rāma rāma rāma harē
harē kṛṣṇa harē kṛṣṇa kṛṣṇa kṛṣṇa harē harē
madhurāpuri sadanā hē vēṇugōpālā

manamōhana madhusūdana vijayagōpālā
vēṇugōpālā gānavilōlā
gānavilōlā venugōpālā
śaranāgata paripālaka vēṇugōpālā

rādhika manōhara	Robber of mind
madana	Cupid
dīnavalsala	Merciful to the meek
bāla	Child
bhakta jana	Devotees
mandara	Heaven
vēṇu	Flute
muralidhara	Bearer of flute
ganavilōla	Swayed by song
madhurāpur	The city of Madhura
sadanā	Dweller
manamōhana	Enchanter of mind
madhusūdana	One who killed the demon Madhu
saranāgata	Refugee
paripālaka	Protector

RAGHUPATI RĀGHAVA

raghupati rāghava rājā rām
patita pāvana sītā rām (2x)
īśvara allāh tere nām
saba kō san mati de bhagavān (2x)
sītā rām sītā rām
baj tu pyāre sītā rām (2x)

hē bhagavān he bhagavān
saba kō san mati de bhagavān (2x)
śrī rām jai rām jai jai rām
śrī rām jai rām jai jai rām

raghupati	Lord of the Raghus
rāghava	Descendent of Raghu
rāja rām	King Rama
patita pāvana	Savior of the fallen
īsvara allah tērē nām	Your name is Ishwara and Allah
baju tu pyāre sīta rām	Chant "Sita Ram"
hē bhagavan	O Lord
saba kō san mati de bhaga-van	Give a good heart to everyone
śri ram jai ram jai jai ram	Hail to Sri Ram

RĀMA BŌLŌ RĀMA BŌLŌ

rāma bōlō rāma bōlō rāma bōlō rām
śrī rāma bōlō rāma bōlō rāma bōlō ram
śrī rām śrī rām
raghupati rāghava rām
śrī rām śrī rām jānaki jīvana rām
śrī rām śrī rām patita pāvana rām

Say "Rama", say "Rama!" Say "Rama", the Lord of the Raghus, Raghava Rama, Sri Rama, the life of Sita, Sri Rama, Who purifies of all sin.

RĀMA PUJĀRI PĀDA VUPAKĀRI

rāma pujāri pāda vupakāri
mahāvīra bajaranga bali

O great warrior Hanuman, You are the one who always resides near Rama's Feet, ever worshipping them.

sat dharmachāri
sat brahmachāri
mahāvīra bajaranga bali

You are a pure brahmachari, ever abiding by dharma (righteousness).

jana guṇa sāgara rūpa vujāgara
mahāvira bajaranga bali

You are an ocean of wisdom and excellent qualities, of beautiful form.

śaṅkara suvana
saṅkata mōcana
mahāvira

You are an incarnation of Shiva who saves us from sorrows and calamities.

kēsari nandana
kali mala bañjana
mahāvīra

O Kesari's Son, You destroy the evils of the Kali Yuga.

rāghava dhūta
jaya hanumanta
mahāvīra

Victory to Hanuman, Rama's envoy.

añjani nandana
asura nikandana
mahāvīra

You are Anjani's Son, the Destroyer of demons.

maṅgala mūrti māruti nandana mahāvīra

You have an auspicious form, O Son of the Wind.

jaya bala bhīma jaya bala dhāma mahāvīra

Victory to You of gigantic strength, the Abode of strength.

sīta rām sīta rām
sīta rām jai sīta rām

RĀMA RĀGHAVA

rāma rāghava
jaya sītā vallabhā

Victory to Rama of the Raghu race, Beloved of Sita!

RĀMA RAHIMA KŌ

rāma rahima kō bhajane vālē
tērē pujāri kṛṣṇa - tērē nām ēk sahāra

tumhi hō gīta tumhi ramāyana
tumhi hō vēda purān - tērē nām ēk sahāra

O Lord Rama, All-merciful,we sing to Thee. Your Names are many, but You are One. You are the Lord of the Gita, the Ramayana, the Vedas and Puranas.

ŚAKTI DĒ BHAKTI DĒ

śakti dē bhakti dē durga mātā
śakti dē bhakti dē durga mātā

O Mother Durga, please bestow shakti (spiritual power), please bestow bhakti (pure devotion).

darśan ki āsha hē
man mērā pyāsā hē
āj mērī ittnīsi
bātt māniyē

My mind is thirsty and longing for darshan. Please consider this supplication, just this much for today.

cārōn ōr andhēra hē
māyā mēm gēra hē
jñān kā diyā man mēn
jalā dījīyē

There is darkness everywhere, and I am immersed in the maya all around me. Please light the lamp of knowledge in my mind.

dukhōm kā sāgar hē
pāpom ka sāgar hē
mērī tutti naiyyā kō
pār kījiye

In front of me is the ocean of worldly misery, the fathomless sea of sins. Please help my dilapidated boat to get across.

ŚAMBŌ MAHĀDĒVA

śambō mahādēva candra cūda
śaṅkara sāmba sadā śiva
gangādhara hara kailāśa nātha
pāhimām pārvati ramana

O Benevolent, Great God who has the moon on His forehead, giver of auspiciousness, the Benevolent, All-auspicious, who bears the Ganges in His locks, the Destroyer, Lord of Mt. Kailash, O protect me, beautiful Lord of Parvati.

ŚAMBHŌ ŚANKARA

śambhō śaṇkara śambhō śaṇkara
śambhō śaṇkara śiva śambhō
śambhō śaṇkara śambhō śaṇkara
śambhō śaṇkara śiva śambhō
indu kalā dhara ganga jaṭā dharā
śambhō śaṇkara gaurīśā
pannaga bhūshaṇa parimaḷa gātrā
pāvana caraṇā paramēśvarā

O Sambu! O Sankara, the Lord of Gouri (Devi), who wears the crescent moon and the Ganges in his matted hair knot, whose ornaments are serpents, whose body is fragrant, whose feet are holy, and who is the Supreme Lord.

ādi dēva dīna janēśa sāmba sadāśiva varada harē
dēvamuni jana sēvita caraṇā śūla pāṇi durita harē

The Primordial God, Lord of the poor, ever united with Mother (Devi), ever auspicious, Bestower of boons, Who steals the ego, Whose feet are worshipped by gods, sages and men alike, Who holds the trident, and Who destroys sorrows.

parvata nandini priya vadana dēvā
mama tāpa hāra tava śaraṇam
karuṇālaya jaya kailāsa vāsā
śaraṇāgata tava pada śaraṇam

Lord, Whose face is endearing to the Daughter of mountains (Devi), Who robs me of my sorrows, You are my refuge. The abode of mercy, victory to You! You Who stay at Mt. Kailasa, I have come to You for shelter. Your feet are my haven.

ŚAMBHŌ ŚAṄKARA UMĀPATĒ

śambhō śaṇkara umāpatē
pāhi śaṅkara paśupatē
nandi vāhana nāgabhūṣanā cāndraśēkharā jadādharā
gangādhāra śiva gauri manōharā pāhi śaṇkāra sadāśiva

O Shiva, Lord of Parvati, protect us. You who are Lord of all created beings, You ride on the bull Nandi and are adorned with snakes. You wear the moon and matted locks on Your crown. The Ganges issues from Your head. O Shiva, Enchanter of Parvati, protect us, ever-auspicious Shiva.

kailāsa vāsa kanaka sabhēśa sundarēśvara viśvēśā
smaśāna vāsā digambarēśā nīlakantā mahādēvā

You dwell on Mt. Kailasa and dance the Cosmic Dance in the Golden Palace. You have an enchanting form and are the Lord of the Universe. You dwell in the cremation ground and Your mantel is the four directions. You are the greatest God, Lord with a blue throat.

triśūladhāra jyōti prakāśa vibhūti sundara paramēśā
nadanamanōharā damarukanādā pārvati ramana sadāśiva

Carrying the trident, shining with radiance, beautiful and covered with ashes, You are the Supreme God and look beautiful dancing and making music on Your drum. You are adored by Parvati and ever auspicious.

ŚAṄKARA ŚIVA ŚAṄKARA

śaṅkara śiva śaṅkara
śiva śaṅkara rūpa mahēśvara
śiva śaṅkara śankara śaṅkara
ōmkāra prīya śiva śaṅkara
kailāsa prīya śiva śaṅkara
natajana prīya śiva śaṅkara
śaṅkara rūpa mahēśvara

O Auspicious Lord Shiva, the Bestower of all good, the Incarnation of the great Lord Sankara, we love You Who manifest as the Primal Sound. We love You Who dwell on lofty Mt. Kailas. We love You, Lord Shiva, Cosmic Dancer and Source of all good.

ŚANKARĪ ŚĀMBHAVĪ

śankarī sāmbhavī
śivaṅkarī abhayankarī
śrī karī kṛpā mayī
mahēśvarī manōharī
pāhi pāhi mahēśī ambē
durgē śivē pāhimām

O Auspicious One, Consort of Shiva, Giver of auspiciousness and fearlessness, Giver of prosperity, Grace embodied, O Great Goddess, Enchantress of the mind, O Mother Goddess, protect me, protect me, O Durga, Consort of Shiva, protect me!

ŚĀNTAMĀYI OZHUKAṬṬE

śāntamāyi ozhukaṭṭe jīvitam - mauna
śāndra samudrattil cēruvān
sāmōdamozhukaṭṭe jīvitam
satcidānanda sindhuvil cēruvān

May the river of life flow serenely to join the Sea of Dense Silence. May the life flow joyfully to reach the Ocean of Existence, Bliss, and Knowledge.

kaṭal jalam mukilāyi mukil jalam mazhayāyi
mazha jalam nadiyāyi ozhukīṭunnaniśam;
irutīram tazhukunnû kadal tēṭi ozhukunnû
pariṇāma pūrttikuḷḷanudhāvanam
anudhāvanam anudhāvanam anudhāvanam

The waters of the sea become the clouds, the water of the clouds transforms into the rains, the rain water becomes the river and flows perennially. It flows, caressing the two banks, in search of the sea, following the course of evolution to it's fullest. The following, the following.

anubhavam akhilavum azhiverātta anubandham
anubhavattikavāṇu jīvitam;
nīḷunnu pinneyum, jīvita vāhini
nīndu nīndorukaṭṭe śāntamāyi
śāntamāyi śāntamāyi

All is experience, the unbroken continuum; life is the totality of experience. The stream of life still flows on. May it flow endlessly, calmly, calmly, calmly.

SAPTA SVARANGAḶKKUM

sapta svarangaḷkkum
mukti nalkīdunna
śuddha vaikhari rūpiṇi

O Mother, You are the pure 'Vaikhari' sound which gives life to the seven musical notes.

citta rāgaṅgaḷe bhasmamākkīṭunna
śakti mantratinte dhāmamē divya
śakti mantratinte dhāmamē

You are the abode of the 'Shakti mantra' which turns all the attachments of the mind to ashes.

āhatanāhata nāda svarūpiṇi sāhitī tīrtta pravāhinī
mānava hṛdayattil āgama saundarya
dhārayozhukkum surārādhitē

You are of the nature of the 'ahata' and 'anahata' sounds (voiced and unvoiced sounds). You are the One who makes the stream of literature flow. You are the One, worshipped even by the Gods, who makes the stream of the revealed scriptures flow in human hearts.

sarasījāyata lōla sulōcanē
tarasā namikkunnitayenmanam

My mind bows down in reverence to You, the lotus-eyed One.

manalaya śantikkāyiozhukaṭṭe
nin puṇya mṛdu gāna rāga sudhāmṛtam

Let Your sacred soft music flow like a stream of ambrosia, and let my mind lose itself in that stream.

ŚĀRADE ŚĀRADE

śārade śārade
divya mahite śārade
śārade śārade
hamsa asane śārade
śārade śārade
māyura gamane śārade
śārade śārade
sakala kalā vāni śārade

Sarasvati, Sarasvati, O Divine Intelligence, Sarasvati, Sarasvati, sitting on a swan, Sarasvati. Sarasvati walking like a peacock, Sarasvati. Sarasvati, You are the repository of the Arts and all branches of learning.

ŚARAṆAM ŚARAṆAM BHAGAVĀNE

śaraṇam śaraṇam bhagavāne
śaraṇāgata vatsalā bhagavāne

Give me refuge, give me refuge, O Lord, Thou who take loving care of all who come to Thy fold!

aṛivillatavarāṇē bhagavānē
āśraya mēkaṇē bhagavānē

We are ignorant, oh Lord, please give us refuge!

maraṇam varayum nin tiru nāmam
mananam ceyyēṇam bhagavāne

Let me reflect on Thy Holy Name until the moment of my death.

kaliyuga varadanām bhagavānē
mama jīvan prāṇanam bhagavānē

Thou art the Bestower of boons in this dark age of materialism. Thou art the very life and the vital energy within me.

kanivōṭu nin pāda paṭmattiṇgaḷ
āśaraṇaneyennennum cērtīṭeṇē

With compassion, kindly give this helpless one refuge at Thy Lotus Feet for ever.

ŚARAṆĀRTHIKALUṬE

śaranārthikaluṭe
kadanaṅgaḷ akattuvān
avatāram kaikonda kāruṇyamē
ammē apāra kāruṇamē

O Mother of boundless compassion, You are Compassion Incarnate, Who has come down among us to ameliorate the pain of those who take refuge in You.

niṟa katiroḷi tūkum kuḷir candrikayāyi
adiyante manassil nī uṇarāvu
karma sukṛtattil amṛtam nī coriyāvû

Like the cool rays of the full moon spreading its fullness everywhere, please shower the nectar of Your bounteous Grace on my inner firmament.

ānanda cinmayē nin sannidhānattil
ñān enna bhāva meṅgō māyunnu
janmavum karmavum prakṛtiyum puruṣanum
ammayānennōruṇma teḷiyunnu

When I bow down to that radiant bliss of Your presence, the feeling of 'me' disappears. Then the understanding dawns on me that birth, karma, the manifested world and the unmanifested Reality are all just so many aspects of my Mother.

ā madhu smitam nukarumbōzhennile
dāhavum mōhavum akalunnu
karaḷnontu viḷichāl amma tan
anugraham kai varumenna satyam aṟiyunnu

All my delusions and thirst fade away, when I savour that sweet smile. And I realise the truth, that Amma's blessing will always come to one who calls from the heart.

SARASIJA NAYANĒ

sarasija nayanē pūrṇa sanātanī
ammē abhayam tarū nī dēvī

oru varam aruḷān varū nī
eriyumen karaḷinu kuḷirēkān kaniyū nī
santāpa śānti tarū nī dēvī

O lotus-eyed One, perfect and perennial, Goddess and Mother, please give me this one boon: let me have some respite from my litany of sorrow; may this burning heart get some cool relief. Please grant me refuge.

sarasvatī vāg dēvatē
vēdāmbikē ammē
amṛtānandamayī mama jananī

O Mother Amritanandamayi, Goddess Sarasvati, Goddess of inspired speech, Mother of the Vedas, my Mother.

ellām ñān enna bhāvattil karmaṅgaḷ
ceytu pōyammē bhava tāriṇī
kara kāṇa kaṭalil jani mṛti cuzhiyil
āndu pōyammē tunaykku nī
karam nīṭṭi kara kēttān kaniyū nī

O Mother, all my actions were done with the sense of 'me, the doer', and such karmas have immersed me in the ocean of worldliness with no shore in sight. They have sunk me in the quick-sand of death, transmigration and rebirth. O Saviour of all, please extend Your hand of assistance, and extricate me from this mire.

vāg dēvatē nin kṛpayālen vākkukaḷ
hitamāyi mitamāyi priyamākaṇam
karmangaḷ sarvavum lokārttamakaṇam
ānanda bhairavi ambikē
amṛtānanda bhairavi ambikē

O Goddess of Learning, through Your Grace, may my speech be pleasant and agreeable to one and all. May my actions benefit the whole world.

SARASVATĪ SARASVATĪ

sarasvatī sarasvatī
sarasija nayanē sarasvatī
vīnā pāni sarasvatī
vēda vilāsini sarasvatī
vidyādāyini sarasvatī varapradāyini sarasvatī
saṅkata hāriṇi
maṅgala kāriṇi sarasvatī
jagadōdhāriṇi sarasvatī
ānanda dāyini sarasvatī

Sarasvati, Sarasvati, O lotus eyed, Sarasvati. Holding the veena, You are blossoming with knowledge of the Vedas, O Sarasvati. You are the Giver of knowledge, the Bestower of boons, O Sarasvati. Destroyer of sorrows, Giver of all good things, O Sarasvati. You uphold the world, Sarasvati. You are the Giver of bliss, O Sarasvati.

ŚIVA ŚIVA HARA HARA

śiva śiva hara hara
śiva śiva hara hara
mēgām bara dhara
damaru sundara hara
śiva śiva hara hara śiva śiva hara hara

O Auspicious One, Destroyer Who is clothed in the clouds, the beautiful one playing the damaru (small drum).

kara triśūla dhara
abhaya suvara hara
bhasma anga dhara
jadā jūda dhara
bāla candra dhara
dīna nayana dhara
nāga hara dhara
munda māla dhara

Who holds the Trident in His hands bestowing fearlessness and boons, Who wears ash on His limbs and has matted locks, Who bears the crescent moon on His forehead, Who has eyes full of compassion, wearing cobras as a garland and a necklace of skulls.

hara hara śiva śiva hara hara
śaṅkara śiva śaṅkara
śiva śambhō mahādēva śaṅkara

O Auspicious One, the Destroyer, the Great God.

ŚIVA ŚIVA MAHĀDĒVA

śiva śiva mahādēva
nama śivāya sadā śiva
kāli kāli mahā mātā
nāma kālikē namō namā
durga durga mahā māyā
nāma durgāya namō namā

śiva	Auspicious One
mahadēva	Great God
nāma	Salutations
sadā	Always

kali	Devi as the Destroyer
mahā mātā	Great Mother
kalikē	Goddess Kali
durga	Devi
mahā māyā	Great Illusion

ŚIVĀYA PARAMĒŚVARĀYA

śivāya paramēśvarāya
saśi śēkharāya nama ōm
bhavāya guṇa sambhavāya
śiva tāndavāya nama ōm
śivaya paramēśvarāya
candra śēkharāya nama ōm

O Shiva, Great Lord Who wears the crest jewel of the crescent moon, obeisance to Thee Who is the embodiment of all virtues, Who performs the celestial Tandava dance.

SKANDĀ MURUGĀ VARUVĀYĒ

skandā murugā varuvāyē
śānti taravē aruḷ vāyē

Welcome, my Skanda (chief of the celestial army), Muruga (One who travels on the peacock). Bless me by granting peace.

kaṇamēnum vārāyi en daivamē
kaṇṇāre kandāl pōtumē
tuṇayāka vantāl ennatayuyirē
nī śōnna paṭiye nānāṭuven

O Lord, come with Your golden trident. If only I could behold You with my eyes, the essence of all the forces of life. Won't You be my companion, O life of my life? According to the tune You play, I will dance.

muruga muruga muruga
entan manam unnai tēṭutē
unten mahimai pāṭutē
enatākki vantāl unatāki vāzhvēn
nī śōnna paṭiye nānāṭuven

Tell me, is life not a dream but to be lived? Bless me with the safe path till the end of my life's journey. My mind searches for You, it sings Your glories. O Lord, come for my sake, I will ever live for You and according to the tune You play, I will dance.

SNĒHAMAYĪ ŚRĪ BHAGAVATĪ

snēhamayī śrī bhagavatī
smitā svarūpiṇi smarāmi satatam
amṛtamayī śrī bhagavatī
smitā svarūpiṇi smarāmi satatam

We remember You always, O Amritamayi, the auspicious Bhagavati (an aspect of Devi, the seat of six great virtues) who is the embodiment of love and smile incarnate.

varadāna lōle varadābhaye dēvi
varavīnā pustaka dhāriṇīyambikē
vidyā pradē viśvēśvarī
varamaruḷuka ñaṅgaḷkku
śrī bhagavatī

Mother Devi, Whose intention is to bestow boons, Who protects and showers fortunes on us, Who holds a fine veena and the scriptures. O Bhagavati, Bestower of knowledge, Empress of the Universe, grant us a boon.

duritaṅgaḷ nīngān
kaniyeṇam ennennum
abhayam nī ñaṅgaḷil coriyeṇam ambikē
karuṇānidhe kaniyēṇamē
varamaruḷuka ñaṅgaḷkku
śrī bhagavatī

Kindly shower Grace on us for the removal of misery and protect us, O Mother! The treasure chest of Grace, have mercy on us and grant us boons.

SNĒHĀMṚTĀNANDINI

snēhāmṛtānandini - amma
svētāmbarādambari
bhāvābhirāmēśvari amma
pārinnu sarvēśvari

ammē amṛtānandamayī
ammē viśvaprēmamayī
ammē amṛtānandamayī
vandē mātā praṇavamayī

kāruṇya pūrṇāmṛtam - snēha
sārātma rūpāmṛtam
kātinnu nādāmṛtam - kannin
ānānda rūpāmṛtam

vēdānta sārāmṛtam – satcid-
ānanda divyāmṛtam
jīvannu jīvāmṛtam - santat
ānanda dhyeyāmṛtam

sanmātra rūpāmṛtam - pūrṇa
brahma svarūpāmṛtam
advaita vidyāmṛtam - jñāna-
sadrūpa nityāmṛtam

snēhamṛtanandini	Loving Mother of immortal bliss
svēthambaradambari	Mother who wears white robes
bhavabhiramēśvari	The Supreme Being of pleasing woods
parinnu sarvēswari	The Supreme Goddess of the Universe
viśvaprēmamayi	Mother of Universal Love
karuṇyapurṇam	Full of compassion
snēhasarātmarūpam	Of the form of the essence of love
kātinnu nādāmṛtam	Music to the ears
kanninnānanda rūpamṛtam	Blissful form to the eyes
vēdanta saramṛtam	The gist of Vedanta
satcidānanda divyamṛtam	Existence, consciousness, bliss absolute
jīvannu jīvamṛtam	Life giving ambrosia to the soul
santatānanda	Ever happy
dhyeyāmṛtam	To be meditated upon
sanmatra rûpamṛtam	Of various forms
purṇabrahma svarūpam	Of the form of Pure Brahma
advaita vidyamṛtam	Non dual knowledge

jnāna sadrūpa nityamṛtam	Ever in the form of knowledge

ŚRĪ KARĪ KRIPĀ KARĪ

śrī karī kṛpā karī
priyankarī sarvēśvarī
śaṅkarī abhayankarī
sumangalī sarvēśvarī
tāndava priya śrī karī
bhairavī pralayankarī
sarvēśvarī sundarī
dayā karī manōharī

śrī	Prosperity
kari	One who bestows
kṛpa	Grace
priyam	That which we love
sarvēśvari	Goddess of all
saṅkari	Auspicious one
abhayankari	Bestower of protection and fearlessness
sumangali	Auspicious (also married one)
tandava priya	Who likes the Cosmic Dance
bhairavi	Consort of Bhairava (Shiva)
pralayam	Cosmic dissolution
sundarī	Beautiful
dayā	Mercy
manōhari	Charming

ŚRI KṚṢṆA CAITANYA

śri kṛṣṇa caitanya
vithale rakumāyi
rādhe śyām pānduranga
rādhe gōvindā

rādhe gōvinda bhaja
rādhe gōpāla
pandari nātha pānduranga
rādhe gōvinda

kṛṣṇa	Allattracting One
caitanya	Consciousness
vithale rakumayi	Lord Vishnu and Lakshmi
rādhe śyam	Radha and Krishna
pānduranga	Of white color
gōvinda	Lord of the cows
gōpala	Cowherd Boy
pandarinātha	Lord of Pandarapur

ŚRI KṚṢṆA GŌVINDA

śri kṛṣṇa gōvinda harē murāre
hē nātha nārāyaṇa vāsudēva
nārāyaṇa nārāyaṇa vāsudēva
nārāyaṇa vāsudēva
hē nātha nārāyaṇa vāsudēva
harē murāre kṛṣṇa harē murāre
harē murāre rāma harē murāre
hē nātha nārāyaṇa vāsudēva

śri kṛṣṇa gōvinda harē murāre
hē nātha nārāyaṇa vāsudēva
kṛṣṇa vāsudeva
gōvinda gōvinda gōvinda vāsudēva
nārāyaṇa nārāyaṇa nārāyaṇa vāsudēva
hē nātha nārāyaṇa vāsudēva

śrī kṛṣṇa	The Glorious Allattracting One
gōvinda	Lord of the cows
harē	Reliever of the distressed
murāre	Destroyer of the demon Mura
hē nātha	O Lord
nārāyaṇa	The One Who rests on the Primal Waters
vāsudēva	In Whom all exists

ŚRĪ MĀTĀ JAGAN MĀTĀ

śrī mātā jagan mātā
ambā mātā śaśi gauri mātā

dhāraṇī mātā paripūranī mātā
jagōdhāriṇī mātā bhavahāriṇī mātā

jagan mātā	Mother of the world
ambā	Mother
sasi gauri	White like the moon
dharaṇī	Support of the universe
paripurani	Perfection
jagōdhariṇi	Substratum of the world
bhavahariṇi	Destroyer of the cycle of becoming

ŚRĪ PĀDA MĀHĀTMYAM

śrī pāda māhātmyam ārkkariyām - guru
pādattin vaibhavamārkkariyām
amṛteśvarī ammē ānanda sāramē
kaivalya dhāmamē ñān namikkām
amṛtēṣvari pādam vandē (2)

Who knows the importance of the lotus feet of the Guru? Who knows the grandeur of the Guru's feet? Amme, Amritesvari, the Essence of bliss, the Abode of Liberation, I am prostrating to You!

śrī pāda pūjakku mēlilla pūjakaḷ
illa yōgādikaḷ sādhanakaḷ
sad guru pādattil prēmavum śraddhayum
janma janmāntara puṇyamallō

There is no worship superior to the worship of the Guru's feet. Yogas, spiritual practices, etc., are all inferior to the Guru's feet! One gets love and alertness from the Satguru's feet due to virtues accumulated during many previous births.

trippāda bhakti sadā kalpa vṛkṣamām
prēma bhakti pradam jñāna mūlam
bhakti mukti pradam sarvva siddhi pradam
śrī pāda tīrttamē tīrttasāram

Devotion to the lotus feet of the Guru is like a wish-fulfilling tree which gives love, devotion and knowledge. The water which washes the Guru's feet is the holiest of all holy waters and grants devotion, liberation and all merits.

sākṣāl anantanum mūrtti trayaṅgaḷum
vākku kiṭṭāte valaññiṭunnu
pinnāru varṇṇikum sadguru pādatte
vīndum namikkām namichiṭām ñān

Even the thousand-tongued serpent Ananta and the Trinity (Brahma, Vishnu and Shiva) find it difficult to glorify the Guru's feet, as they run out of words. This being so, who else is there to describe properly the feet of the Guru? I am prostrating to You again and again!

ŚRĪ RĀMACANDRA

śrī rāmacandra raghu rāmacandra
prabhu rāmacandra bhagavān
śrī dhanya dhanya sītābhirāma
sukṛtātma rūpa rāmā

O Sri Ramachandra, Thou of Raghu's dynasty, Lord Ramachandra, O God, the blessed and auspicious Beloved of Sita, Whose Form is the very soul of the pious

hē jānaki ramaṇa rāghava vimala vīra sūrya kūla jātā
hē rāma rāma raghuvīra rāma
karunārdra nētra rāma
śrī rāma rāma jaya rāma rāma
jaya rāma rāma jaya rāmā

O Delighter of Sita (Janaki), taintless One who was born in the dynasty of the Sun and glorified for His strength and bravery, O Rama, with eyes moistened by compassion

hē mauktika bharana būṣitā
bhuvana saundaryātma jaya rāma

ānanda rūpa nīgamānta sāra
nikhilātma rūpa rāma
śrī rāma rāma jaya rāma rāma
jaya rāma rāma jaya rāma

O Rama Who wears ornaments of pearl, Who is the Jewel of the world, Bliss Incarnate, the Quintessence of the Upanishads, the integral form of all souls

ŚRĪ LALITAMBIKĒ SARVA ŚAKTĒ

śrī lalitāmbikē sarva śaktē
śrī lalitāmbikē sarva śaktē
śrī lalitāmbikē sarva śaktē
śrī pādam ñānitā kumbiṭunnen

O Sri Lalitambika, You are the All-powerful. I humbly prostrate to Your Divine feet.

taranam enikku guṇangaḷ sarvam
śaraṇam gamichoru
dukkhitan ñān
tēru tere vīṇu vaṇaṅgīṭuvān
oru poṭi kāruṇyam ēkiṭēnē

Please give me all virtues. I am miserable and seek refuge in You. Please grant me just a little of Your Grace so that I may always have devotion to Your Lotus Feet.

tava kaṭakkannināl onnu nōkki
mama khēdam okke ozhikka dēvī
aviṭutte dāsiye kākkukillē
alivezhānentinī ceytiṭēṇam

Please look at me with Your compassionate eyes and remove all my sorrows. Please take care of this servant of Yours. What can I do to melt Your heart?

arutarutamme tyajichiṭollē
śaraṇamagaṭikku nalkiyālum
gamanattilamma nayichiṭenam
gati vēṟeyillā śaraṇamammē

Please don't leave me. Please grant me refuge. Please guide me on my journey. I have nobody else.

akhila kāmaṅgaḷum nalkum ammē
karuṇayērīṭum mahēśi bhadrē
mananam ceytīṭānāyi śakti nalkū
manatāril nityavum nṛttamāṭū

Please grant me all boons, O compassionate Mother. Please grant me the strength to meditate. Please dawn eternally in my heart.

oru nūru janmam kazhiññ tāvām
taruṇattil marttyanāyi tīrnnatākām
viraḷamāyi tanneyī janmammē
padamalar kumbiḷil nalkiṭaṭṭe

Even though I have had hundreds of births before gaining a human form, I offer this body at Your lotus feet.

pizhakal adhikamāyi ceytirikkām
tanayaril ñān nindya nāyirikkām
jananī nī ellām kshamichivante
manatāpamokkey akattitenam

Although I have committed many mistakes and am a worthless son/daughter, Mother, please forgive me and remove my anguish.

jñānamō śāstramō yōgamō nī
ēkiyiṭṭillennatōrmma vēṇum
oru karmavum tiriyāttorenne
calanappeṭuttunna tentināṇu

Please remember that You have not given me special knowledge of the scriptures or of meditation. Why are You creating such sorrow for one who doesn't even understand the workings of Karma?

śariyāyi nayikkuvān ārumillā
toru śōka sāmrājyam uḷḷilenti
iṭayiṭe tēṅgaḷ dhvanikaḷumāyi
aṭiyan tavātmaja ettiṭunnu

There is nobody to guide me. I come to You with a heart full of sorrow and anguish.

mama mātāvum pitāvum guruvum
manavṛkṣa puṣpa phalavum amma
ninavukaḷ okkeyum ninnilākān
kanivu nalkīṭuvān kai tozhunnen

Oh, Mother, You are my father, mother, teacher and the fruits of all actions. I will think only of You. Please show compassion to me.

kēra vṛkṣaṅgaḷe vallikaḷe
niṅgaḷ endammaye kandatundō
pon tārakaṅgaḷe niṅgaleṅgān
entamma pōyatu kandatundō

Have you seen my Mother, oh coconut trees and climbers? Oh golden stars, have you seen where my Mother has gone?

rākkiḷi kūṭṭame niṅgaḷeṅgān
entamma tan vazhi kandatundō
hē niśāgandhi nī kanduvō col
entamma yī vazhi pōyatundō

Oh, nightingales, do you know the way She went? Hey, nightblooms, have you seen Her?

ōrō kaṭalkkara tōṛum ammē
ninne tiraññu karaññidum ñān
ōrō maṇal tariyōṭum ammē
ninne kuṛichu tirakkiṭum ñān

I will look for You on every seashore and will enquire about You from every particle of sand.

nīyallā tillārumeṅgaḷkkammē
nī tanne śvāsa nīśvāsamennum
ninne piriññu kazhiññiṭānō
ñaṅgaḷkkoralpavum vayyā tāyē

Who is there for us except You? You are our very breath. We cannot live without You.

nī pin tiriññu naṭannu vennāl
potti takarnnitum ñaṅgaḷamme
ninne pirinyor arakṣanavum
ñaṅgaḷ sahichīdukilla tāyē

If You abandon us we will be shattered. We can't be apart from You for even a second.

ammē ponnamme prakāśame nī
prēmāmṛtam tūki vāzhaname
mānasa nētram teliññu nilkkum
hṛdayākāśattil nī vāzhaname

My dear Mother of light, stay forever in our hearts and bless us with the nectar of Eternal Bliss.

ninne pirinyoru nēramammē
vayya vayyottum kazhiññiṭuvān
nī maraññiṅgane ninnitūkil
ninne tiraññu ñān māttayākum

I cannot live without You. I will go crazy looking for You if You go on hiding like this.

minnāminuṅgē prakāśa muttē
rāvin vēḷichamē nillu nillu
amma tan dūti nī ennu tōnnum
nīyeṅgāne entamme kandatundō

Oh, fireflies, lights of the night, you look like messengers from my Mother. Have You not seen Her?

māzhkiṭum ambala prāvukaḷe
entammayī vazhi pōyatundō
ambalatinnuḷḷil pāttu kānum
ambala dīpame collu collu

Oh, wailing temple birds, did you see my Mother go this way? Is She hiding in the temple?

yuga yugāntaṅgaḷāyi ñān alaññu
yuga yugāntaṅgaḷayi nī maraññu
karuṇāmayī ninakkentū patti
karuṇa kāṭṭīṭān amāntamentē

I have wandered for ages and You have stayed away for ages, Oh merciful One. What happened to You? Why are You delaying in bestowing Your grace?

vayya vayyāmmaye kandiṭāte
nīṛi nīṛittane nīṅgiṭuvān
amma tan mārgam paṛaññiṭuvān
ārārum illayō collu collu

I can't go on living without Mother and I have none to show me the way to Her.

prēma mūrtte ninakkentu patti
nin kṛpā sindhu varandu pōyō
ninne piriññu ñān etra kālam
iniyum alayaṇam colka tāyē

O Love Incarnate, has Your ocean of mercy run dry? How long will I have to wander without You?

ninte kāruṇyam labhichiṭuvān
ñān entu vēlayum ceyyum ammē
ninne labhichidum vēla tanne
vēlayenna muni śrēṣṭha rōti

I will do anything to gain Your compassion. The seers have said true action is only done to gain You.

entu ninakku santōshamāṇō
innatu ceytiṭām ente tāyē
onnonnu mātram innente ichcha
nin maṭi taṭṭilī kuññirikkum

Whatever pleases You I will do. My only desire is to be on Your lap.

ninne labhichiṭum cinta cinta
ninne labhichiṭum karmam karmam
ninne labhichiṭum dharmam dharmam
ninne labhichiṭum dhyānam dhyānam

Thoughts to gain You are the only real thoughts; actions to gain You are the only real karma; duty to gain You, is the only real dharma and meditation to attain You is the only real meditation.

cintakaḷ okkeyum ninte cinta
karmangaḷ okkeyum ninte pūja
nin nāmam colluvān cundanaṅgum
nī mātram ammē enikku sarvam

All my thoughts are about You, all my actions are worship offered at Your feet; my lips move only to chant Your divine name; I have only You as my All in all.

nīyente munnil innettiṭēṇam
śrī pādam kaṇṇīril mukkiṭēṇam
nin prēma bhakti en ātma nādam
mattonnum entamme vēnda vēnda

Please come to me so I can wash Your blessed feet with my tears. I don't want anything except loving devotion to You.

nīyenne viṭṭiṭṭin ōṭiṭēndā
ninne uruṭṭi piṭichiṭum ñān
nāmam japicheṛiññinnu ninne
ñān ente kayyil kurukkum ammē

You won't be able to leave me anymore. I am holding tightly onto You by chanting Your Divine Name.

itrayum nāḷenne viḍḍiyākki
innini appaṇi vēnda durgē
nī ente śvāsamāyi tīrnnupōyi
nīyente prāṇante prāṇanāyi

Oh Durga don't play Your tricks and abandon me again. You are my very breath, You are my life itself.

ente hṛt spandanam ninnilallō
en cintayellām ninnuḷḷil allō
ñān tanne ninte maṭiyil allō
tārāṭṭu pāṭān maṛanniṭolle

My heart beats within You and my thoughts are within You. I am in Your lap; please don't forget to sing me a lullaby.

ā pāṭṭil muṅgi mayaṅgiṭām ñān
sacchidānandam nukarnneṇīkkām
ennekkum en nidra tīrnninṭaṭṭe
entammayil ñān unarnniṭaṭṭe

I will wake up forever. My sleep will be over forever and I will be enlightened in my Mother.

SUKHAMEṆṆI TIRAYUNNA

sukhameṇṇi tirayunna manujā ninnabhimānam
veṭiyāte bhūvanattil
sukham enginī
dayā rūpi jagadamba akatāril teḷiyāte
manujā nin manassinnū sukham ētini

You who search all around for happiness, how can you get it without shedding your vanity? How can you be happy until the compassionate Mother of the Universe shines in your heart?

parābhakti uṇarātta manujante manamennum
maṇāmatta malarinnu samamāyi varum
iḷakunna kaṭalinte alayilpeṭṭila pōle
duritattiluzharītān iṭayāyi varum
janimṛtiyil peṭṭalayānāy iṭayāyi varum

The mind in which devotion for the Supreme Power is not alive is like a flower without fragrance. Such a mind will be forced to toss around in misery like a leaf tossed by the waves of the restless ocean.

vidhi enna kazhukante nakharattil amarāte
vijanattil irun ātma bhajanam ceyyū
phalam eṇṇi tirayāte satatam tan manatāril
sakalātma rūpiye bhajanam ceyyū - sakala
duritam pōy sukhamēlān iṭayāy varum

Do not get caught in the talons of the vulture known as fate. Worship the Self in seclusion. Stop searching for results everywhere and worship the form of the Universal Self in the blossom of the heart!

SUNDARA KAṆṆĀ KAṆṆĀ

sundara kaṇṇā kaṇṇā vandita rūpa
nanda kumāra kaṇṇā mañjula hāsā
pāvana nāma kaṇṇā pāpa vināśa
pāhi pāhi mām kaṇṇā pālaya saure
kaṇṇā kaṇṇā kaṇṇā kaṇṇā

O beautiful Kanna (Krishna), with a form that inspires the mood of worship, the son of Nanda, with a captivating smile — Kanna, the Destroyer of imperfection, Whose Name is hallowed, please protect me.

vēṇugōpālā kaṇṇā vēda svarūpā
gāna vilōlā kaṇṇā gōkula nātha
gōpa kumāra kaṇṇā gōpī vallabhā
rāsa vilōlā kaṇṇā rājiva lōcana
kaṇṇā kaṇṇā kaṇṇā kaṇṇā

O lotus-eyed Venugopala, Who embodies the Truth of the Vedas, Lover of music, and the Lord of Gokula — the gopis adore You and You love the divine sport of Rasa.

kamala lōcana kaṇṇā kāruṇya rūpā
kadana nāśana kaṇṇā kamsa mardanā
madana mōhanam kaṇṇa tavakāṇanam
tāvaka nāmam kaṇṇā tāpa nāśanam
kaṇṇā kaṇṇā kaṇṇā kaṇṇā

O lotus-eyed Kanna, Compassionate one, Destroyer of sorrow, Slayer of Kamsa, Your face is enchanting and Your very Name annihilates my suffering.

SUNDARI NI VĀYŌ

sundari ni vāyō purandari ni vāyō
śaṅkari ni vāyō nirandari ni vāyō

Come, O Beautiful One who destroys sorrow. Come, O Consort of Shiva, who surpasses the three states of being. Come, Auspicious One. Come, O Eternal One.

kandan tandaukku vāmākṣi nī ennum
kānti pūrate cintum kāmakṣi nī
bandhuvāyi kānmōrkku
svantam nīye en cindaykku
uravāyi ninnīdamma

Thou art the Eternal Consort of Shiva, Father of Muruga. Thou art Kamakshi, the Lustrous One. For those who look upon Thee as their dear relation, Thou art their own. O Mother, please remain as the spring of all my thoughts.

onnāyi palatāyi arūpavumāyi
ninnālum jyōtirmayi
brahmam nīyē
nannāyenuḷḷam nī aṟiyillayō
connālum munnil
nī varukillayō

Thou art Brahman, the Self-luminous, and unique as well as the multitude of forms and formless, too. Doesn't Thou knowest my Inner Self? Won't Thou come before me when I call?

SVĀMI ŚARAṆAM AYYAPPA

svāmi śaraṇam ayyappa
śaraṇam śaraṇam ayyappa
svāmi śaraṇam ayyappa
śaraṇam śaraṇam ayyappa

ayyappa	Name for the Lord Progeny of Shiva and Vishnu
śaraṇam	Refuge
svāmi	Lord

śrī śabarīśa svāmi
śaraṇam ayyappā
ārthivināśa svāmi
śaraṇam ayyappā
sāśvata mūrtte svāmi
śaraṇam ayyappā
māmala vāsā svāmi
śaraṇam ayyappā

Lord of Sabari a tribal woman greatly devoted to Rama. Sabarimala is the mountain on which she lived and which is the site of the famous Ayyappa temple. Destroyer of greed, the Form Eternal, Dweller on the Mountain, O Lord Ayyappa, Thou art my refuge.

caranarenu śirasilaniññu
paramabhakti manasil viriññu
paramaśānti parannozhukum
tirupādamalar teḷiññukandu
nayanasukham varane svāmi
hṛdayalayam varane
aruṇakkuravidame svāmi
paramapādam tarane

By wearing the dust of Thy Feet on the head, with supreme devotion in the mind, by holding onto the clear vision of Thy Feet, from where gush out perfect peace, let the eyes enjoy pleasure and let the heart melt away. Lord, the Source of Mercy, please deliver me to the Supreme State.

pāpam tīrān tāpam tīrān
janimṛti dukham asēṣam tīrān
pati patinettum kayaripparichil
paramātmāvin tatvam
urakkān oru varan arulaṇame svāmi
padamalar tuna taranē
akamalar uṇarvu varān svāmi
kanivamṛtarulaṇamē

To exhaust sin, to end grief, and to wash off completely the sorrow of births and deaths, to climb up the eighteen steps leading to the temple at Sabarimala and to understand firmly and quickly the principle of the Supreme Self, kindly bless us, Lord, kindly have mercy on us.

ŚYĀM RĀDHE ŚYĀM (ĀRATI KUÑJAVIHARI)

śyām rādhe śyām rādhe
śyām rādhe śyām
rādhe śyām rādhe śyām
rādhe śyām rādhe śyām

āratī kuñjavihāri kī
śrī giridhara kṛṣṇa murāri kī
śyām rādhe śyām

This is the arati for Lord Krishna Who lives in the bower, for the One Who killed the demon Mura and held the mountain aloft on His hand.

galē mē vaijayanti mālā
bajāve murali madhura bālā
śravana mē kuṇḍala chala kālā

He wears a garland of wild flowers on His neck and is the Boy Who sweetly plays the flute, the One with the swinging kundala ear pendants.

nanda kē nanda hē nanda lālā
śrī giridhara kṛṣṇa murāri kī
śyām rādhe śyām
gagan sam angakānti kārī
vilāsa sab parta nind chāli
bhramara sam ālak
kastūrī tilak candra sam damak
lalita chavi śyām pyāri kī
śrī giridhara kṛṣṇa murāri kī
śyām rādhe śyām

He is the dear Son of Nanda, with a body lustrous as a dark rain cloud, with eye shadow as dark as a black bee, cooling as the moon, having a tilak of musk, slender, affectionate and beautiful, the One Who killed the demon Mura and held the mountain aloft on His hand.

ŚYĀMNE MURALĪ

śyāmne muralī madura bajāyi,
vajayi, muralimadhu bajayi
nirmala jīvan jamunā jal me
lahar lahar laharāyi, śyāmne

Krishna played a sweet tune on the flute which thrilled my heart like the waves on the pure waters of the Yamuna.

nirmal gagan pavan nirmal hē
nirmal dharttikā āchal hē
nirmal he tan nirmal hē man
nirmal ras kī ras rachāyi

The sky is clear, the wind is gentle, the face of the earth is clean. People are healthy physically and mentally. All is due to the divine dance of the Lord.

nirmal svar me vēṇu pukāre
vrishaba sune vraj rajkumāri
nirmal lōcan nirmal chitt van
manme nirmal lagan lagāyi

The flute is calling with a divine tune. The cows, children of Vraj and all of the surrounding area are singing to this tune with their heart fully concentrated.

TAKE ME AWAY

Take me away won't you carry me
Let me rest in your arms for a while

Take me away won't you carry me
Let me bathe in the sweetness of your smile

Mother take me away, Mother take me away

TĀMARA KAṆṆĀ VARŪ

tāmara kaṇṇā varū kṛṣṇā guruvāyūrappā
rādhāramaṇā gōpī kṛṣṇā
nityam ninne kāttirippū

O lotus-eyed One, Krishna, Lord of Guruvayur, come! O Radha's Lord, Gopi Krishna, I am constantly waiting for You.

tāi dēvaki paramānandamē
ennu nalkum nī nin darśanam
mayilpīli muṭi cūṭi
maññayum cutti
candanam cārtti
pon cilaṅkakaḷ keṭṭi
ōmana kaṇṇā śrī kṛṣṇā
ōṭakkuzhalumāyi ōṭivarū

O Supreme Bliss of Devaki (Krishna's mother), when will You grant me Your vision? With Your hair decorated with peacock feathers, dressing Yourself in yellow robes, with sandalwood paste on Your forehead, wearing golden anklets, with the flute in Your hands, come running, darling Krishna!

bhaktayām mīrayuṭe sangītamē
kēḷkkunnuvō nī en stutikaḷ
saptasvaraṅgaḷum rāgavum śrutiyum
tāḷavum bhāvavum layavum nīyē
gandharva gāyakā śrī kṛṣṇā ōmkāra nādam pāṭi varū

O music of Your devotee Meera, don't You hear my hymns? You are the seven notes of music, the different scales, melody, harmony, symphony, rhythm, and mood. O Celestial Singer, Sri Krishna, come, singing the song of OM.

TĀNANA TĀNANĀ

tānana tānanā tanānā tane
tānana tānanā tanānā
tānana tānanā tanānā tane
tānana tānanā tanānā

(This song is the sound of joy as Devi approaches.)

TAN MAN KĪ PUṢPĀÑJALI

tan man kī puṣpāñjali lēkkar
tava caraṇōm mē āyā mā
lē lō sab kuch is jīvan kā
tum kō śīś caḍāyā mā (2x)

O Mother, I have come to know Your lotus feet. Take my body and mind as flower offerings. I have taken refuge in You. Please accept my entire life.

gahar andhērā rāh dikhēnā
ṭhokar pag pag lāgē mā

ban āśā kī kiraṇ sunahari
path ālōkit kardē mā

Being very dark, the path is not visible. I am stumbling at each step. O Mother, please shed light on the path.

kṣudr viṣay sukh jantu bahut hē
vimukh karē man tumsē mā
sañchārit kar bhāv bhakti kā
pal pal prēm pravāhō mā

Many are those who are slaves of trivial pleasures. O Mother, turn my mind away from them. Kindle in me the nature of devotion and let love for You flow unceasingly each and every moment.

mē tum kā yē bhēd vikaṭ hē
ye dīvār bhīch mē mā
dūr karō sab vismṛti dūri
nij āñchal mē lēlō ma

The differentiation between "I" and "You", this wall between "You" and "I" is confusing. Removing the distance between "You" and "I" let me remain forever in Your arms.

TĀYE MAHĀ MĀYĒ

tāyē mahā māyē jananī
jaga jananī

O Mother Mahamaya, Creatrix of the Universe!

japikkunnēn tava nāmam sadā
japikkunnēn tava nāmam

I repeat Your Divine Name constantly, without a break.

mātāvum nī pitāvum nīyē
san mārgam kāṭṭi tarum satguruvum nī

You are my Mother, You are my Father, You are also the Satguru that shows the true path.

ādiyum nīyē antavum nīyē
sarva carāchara pālaki nīyē

You are the beginning, You are the end. You are the One that takes care of all that is in creation, all moving and unmoving things.

kartyāyani dēvī karuṇāmayi ammē
nin pādam namippān anugrahamēkaṇē

O Goddess Katyayani, Compassionate Mother, please bless me that I may bow down to Your Holy Feet.

TIRUKATHAKAḶ PĀDAM

tirukathakal pādam ñān
oru varam nī tāyō
tirukathakaḷ pāṭum nēram
mama hṛdi nī vāyō
oru varam tāyō
mama hṛdi vāyō

Let me sing the glories of Thy holy acts. Please give me a boon. When I sing of Thy glories, please come to my heart.

durgatikaḷ dûrekkaḷayū
durgā bhagavati kāḷī
tvad rūpam kāṇāṇāyi
arthikkunnivan ennum

Remove the ill fate, O Goddess Durga, O Kali. Everyday I beg to have a vision of Thy form.

dhyānattin vazhiyaṛiyillē
gītattinu srutiyillē
mōdattil muzhukānāyi
vēdapporuḷē kaniyū

I do not know the method of meditation, nor is there melody in my music. Have mercy on me and let me immerse myself in bliss, O Essence of the Vedas.

gāyatri kīrttī mukti
kārtyāyani haimavatī
mōkṣātmikayāṇ ennammē
dākṣāyani śaraṇam śaraṇam

Thou art Gayatri, Keerti (fame), Mukti (Liberation), Kartyayani, Haimavati, and Dakshayani (all names of Devi). Thou art the very soul of Realization and the sole refuge.

tatvangaḷ kathaṇam ceyyān
śakti tarū dēvi
viśvamayī nī yilleṅkil
śivan illen aṛiyunnen

Devi, give me power to speak on the essential ideas. I understand that without Thee, the embodiment of the universe, Shiva the Causative Principle, exists no more.

TIRU VAḶḶIKKĀVIL

tiru vaḷḷikkāvil amma śaraṇam - un
trippāda darśanamē śaraṇam
uḷḷam tavittu varam kēḷppavarkku
aḷḷi koṭukkum ammā śaraṇam

O Holy Mother of Vallikkavu, we seek refuge in You. The darshan of Your holy Feet is our refuge. We seek shelter in the Mother, who gives in abundance to all those who seek Her with a burning heart.

kali kāla vēdanaṅgaḷ tāṅkamal
tavikkum māniṭa idayaṅkaḷil
aruloḷi parappi śānti aḷittiṭum
kārttika dīpamē nīyē śaraṇam

O Mother, You are the Kartika Lamp*, who sets the flame of Knowledge alight in the hearts of those who find the burdens of the Kali Yuga (Age of Materialism) unbearable. We seek refuge in You, who alone can give us peace.

*Note: Lighting the Kartika Lamp is an important annual religious festival in some parts of Southern India.

un mayil varṇṇa uruvattai kandu
attaikalam teṭum aṭiyavarkku
kaṇkanda daivamāyi kāzhchi aḷittiṭum
amṛtānanda mayī nīyē śaraṇam

O Amritanandamayi, we seek refuge in Thee who are the visible form of the Goddess, who gives darshan to all those devotees who are thirsty for peace. We love to behold Your peacock-hued dark form.

TVAMĒVA MĀTĀ

tvamēva mātā ca pītā tvamēva
tvamēva bandhus ca sakhā tvamēva
tvamēva vidyā dravinam tvamēva
tvamēva sarvam mama dēva dēva

Thou art my Mother and Father art Thou, Thou art my relative and friend art Thou, Thou art my learning and wealth art Thou, and Thou art my All, my Lord of Lords.

UNARUṆARŪ

unaruṇarū amṛtānādamayī
unarū jaganmātē
tuyilūṇarū jagad jananī
ulakūṇarttān uṇarūnarū

Awaken, awaken, O Mother Amritanandamayi! Awaken World Mother! O Great One, wake up to awaken the world!

parama jyōti param poruḷē
parama bhaktikkaṭimāyāle
hṛdayadēśa kōvilile
maṇi viḷakkē jvalikkya sattē

O Supreme Light, O Supreme Essence, O Thou who art subservient to supreme devotion, O Thou who resides in the temple of the heart as the golden light, deign to shine forth!

taṇu pavanan kuḷi kazhiññū
niṛa veḷicham kizhakku vechū
praṇavamōtī pāṛavakaḷum
brahmamayī uṇarunarū

After bathing, the cool breeze has kindled the light in the east and the birds are singing "OM", the Primordial Sound. Wake up, O Absolute Being, wake up!

ninakkīrikkān orukki vacha
hṛdayamellām iviṭeyallō
pakaliravum kāttukēzhum
makkaḷellām iviṭe yallō

The hearts here are prepared to enshrine Thee, are all here.
Thy children who cry for Thee day and night, are all here.

UṢAKĀLA NĒRAM

uṣakāla nēram tuṣābindu kandā
niśāgandhiyōṭaṭu cōdikkāyi
khēdippatentu nī śōbha prasūnamē
cārattinnillayō nin jananī?
cārattinnillayō nin jananī?

Seeing the dewdrop tears on the Nisagandhi, (a fragrant flower which blooms at night) the Dawn asked, "Why do you worry, radiant flower? Is not your Mother near you?

khēdikka vēnda nī bhārichanāl ñanāl
snēha labhatināyi tapassirunnû
gaunichatillamma dainyata kandannu
karmukilēṟe kaṇṇīrozhukki
karmukilēṟe kaṇṇīrozhukki

Don't be sad. I also did austerities for gaining love during sorrow-filled days with a heavy heart. Mother ignored me. Seeing my miserable condition, the darkened clouds shed many tears.

dāhichirunna ñān nētrāśrudhāraye
pānam tuṭarnnalpa śānti nēṭi
bhīrutvamārnnilla, dhīratvamōṭinnum
teṭunnu ñānā dayāsāgaram
teṭunnu ñānā dayāsāgaram

Being thirsty, I drank all the streams of tears and gained some peace. I didn't become a coward. With bravery, even today, I look for that ocean of love.

bhēdam veṭiññini sōdaratvēna nām ā
prēmātma vāridhikkāyi bhajikkām
snēhamāyi vannamma namme tuṇaykkāykil
antyattōḷam namukkārttu kēzhām
antyattōḷam namukkārttu kēzhām

Forgetting all differences, in the spirit of brotherhood, let us sing the praises of that Ocean of Love. If Mother won't come with love to help us, let us cry till the end.

VĀṬIKOZHIÑETRA

vāṭikozhiñetra 'innale' inninte
vāṭiyil kōrittarikunna pūkkaḷe
māṭiyunarttuvān vīndum taḷirta pū
cūṭuvān 'nāḷeykku' nīrājanōtsava
māṭuvān arṣā bhimāna muṇarññu pōyi

How many yesterdays have withered away and fallen off? In order to wake up horripilating flowers, to wear the newly blossomed flowers, to celebrate the festival of vesper services for "tomorrow", the Vedic pride has been awakened.

maṇṇin sugandham svadikkunna pāmpum
uḷkaṇṇin vēḷicham nukarnna yōgindranum
onnil viṣam viśva dhāhakan yōgitan
uḷḷil tuḷumbunnu snēhāmṛtarnavam
eṅgum pukaḷ konda pālāzhiyā, mṛtam

Look at the snake which enjoys the smell of the earth and the saint who has enjoyed the inner light. In the former, there is world-destroying poison. The latter's mind is full to the brim with the ocean of unalloyed bliss, like the famous ambrosia of the milky ocean.

pālāzhiyil paḷḷikoḷḷum param poruḷ
ezhāzhi cûzhum apāratayikkappuram
minnunnattin puṇya darśanam sadguru
vandya padāmbuja dvandva mennōrttuṣa
sandyakaḷ tōrum namikka bhaktyādaram

The glory of the Lord resting in the milky ocean (of the mind) is immensely greater than the seven seas. Knowing that such greatness can be seen by the darshan of the holy feet of the Guru, I am prostrating at His feet both at dawn and dusk.

kaṇṇinu karppura kāntiyāyi kātukaḷ
kaññûna gānamāyi, nāvinnamṛtāmāyi
gandhamāyi, gāḍānurāga samśleṣamāyi
andatā misram piḷarnnīrnnezhum divya
bandhurā kāramāyi minnunna sadguru

Eyes achieved camphor brilliance, ears began hearing continuous music, the tongue tasted sweet ambrosia, there arose a sweet aroma, for the sense of touch there was a warm, loving embrace. Satguru shines as a brilliant form, destroying all darkness of illusion.

pañchēndriyaṇgaḷkku mappuṛam vākkinnu
sañcari cīṭuvān ākā tōrad bhūtā
piñja jālōjvala bhavyānubhūtitan
veṇtiṅkaḷāyiram cuzhnuyarnettunna
'pañcākṣarī mantra' sāramaṇen guru

My Satguru is beyond the reach of the five senses. His words can reach there. My Satguru is the giver of the five-syllabled mantra which stands as bright as thousands of moons.

VĀK DĒVATĒ VARŪ

vāk dēvatē varū varamaruḷū vara
vīṇa gāna svaramutirū
vēda vadinī dhyeya rūpiṇi
svānta samśōdhinī varū

Come, O Goddess of Speech, and give us a boon. Play on the veena a stringed instrument fine melodies of music. Come, Speaker of the Vedas, the Object of meditation and the Remover of sorrow.

antara mizhi tēṭum nigamāntaporuḷē
āmaya veyilattum surataru taṇaḷē
svara nandini mama daivamē
suralōka jana pūjitē dēvi

Devi, my Goddess, Thou art the One sought by the inner eyes as the essence of Vedic Truth, the shadow of the heavenly tree that comforts one weary of the hot sun of sorrow, the Daughter of Melody and the One worshipped by the celestial beings.

prapañca vēdiyen hṛdaya vēdi
hṛdaya vēdi nin naṭana vēdi
naṭamāṭi vā śruti pāṭi vā
varadāna kutukānanē dēvi

The universal drama is being enacted on the stage of my heart which is the platform for Thee to dance. Come with the dancing steps, humming a tune, Thou, Who art ever desirous of offering benevolent boons.

VARU MURALI MŌHANĀ

varu murali mōhanā kaṇṇa
varu murali mōhanā
pīlikal cārti orukkām tāmara
mizhikaḷil añjana mezhutām
kuṟnira cinniya nettiyil ñān oru
malayaja tilakamaṇikkām kaṇṇa

Come, Kanna with Thine alluring flute. I will adorn Thee with peacock feathers and line those lotus eyes with eye-shadow. Kanna, I will apply a dot of sandalwood paste on Thy forehead bedecked with scattered hair locks.

varavana mālakal cārttām kāñcana
tarivaḷa kāñciyaṇīkkām
kiṅkini keṭṭi naṭattām kālttaḷa
kiṅkila māṭi rasikkām kaṇṇa

I will put on Thee beautiful garlands made of wild flowers, golden bangles and a waistband. I will let Thee walk with tinkling sound.

taḷarukil veṇṇa yorukkam karaḷil
maṇi malar metta virikkām
pularukil ninne viḷikkām atuvare
puḷakitamennil layikkām kaṇṇa

If Thou art tired, I will prepare butter for Thee and lay down a flowery bed within my heart. I will awaken Thee when it is dawn. Until then, O Kanna, remain absorbed in my thrilled self.

VARUNNENNU TŌNNUNNU

varunnennu tōnnunnu
varadāyakan ente
hṛdaya mandirattinte naṭayiletti
ētō nigūḍhamām snēha nīrdhārayil
nīntān tuṭaṅgunnen svāntamippoḷ
aharnniśam ātmāvil avaneyōrttirunnupōyi
karutiyilloru piṭi aval pōlum ñān
varunnēram oru vastu karutāte maruvukil
karuṇāmayan kṛṣṇanentu tōnum?

I think my boon-giver is coming. He has reached in front of the temple of my heart. My mind is swimming (immersed) in the stream of unknown love. Always I sat, thinking of him. I didn't keep even a handful of parched rice with me. What will the merciful Lord Krishna think if I don't keep anything with me when He comes?

karunārdra mānasanallē mukil varṇṇan?
pari bhavikkillāyirikkyām kaṇṇan
itāyiṅgu vanetti, vannennu tōnnunnu
pītāmbarattin praśōbha kandō?

Is not the heart of the dark cloud-hued Lord merciful? Kannan will not mind it. Yes, He has come here already - I think He has come. Did you see the brightness of His yellow attire?

ātmārppanam ceytetirēlkkum ñānappōḷ
āśīrvadikkātirikkillavan
bhagavadppādaṅgalen mizhinīrāl kazhukumbōḷ
karuṇanīr tūkātirikkillavan

I will welcome Him by self-surrender. (Surely He will bless me). When I bathe His divine feet with my tears, I am sure He will shower mercy on me.

VEṄKATARAMAṆĀ

veṅkataramaṇā veṅkataramaṇā
veṅkataramaṇā saṅkataharaṇā
yēdukuṇḍalā veṅkataramaṇā,
vāsudēva veṅkataramaṇā
vāsudēva, vāsudēva, vāsudēva
veṅkataramaṇā
vāsudēva vāsudēva veṅkataramaṇā
śrīnivāsa śrīnivāsa veṅkataramaṇā

viṭhalā viṭhalā viṭhalā viṭhalā
vāsudēva vāsudēva veṅkataramaṇā
śrīnivāsa śrīnivāsa veṅkataramaṇā

rām jinkā nām hē
ayōdhyā jinkā dhām he
aisē raghu nandan kō
hamāra bhi praṇām hē

pāṇḍuranga nām hē
paṇḍaripura dhām hē
aisē dayā sāgar kō
hamāra bhi pranām hē
viṭhalā viṭhalā

veṅkataramaṇa	One who resides on the beautiful hill of Venkata
śrinivāsa	The one in whom Lakshmi resides

yēdukundala	One who resides in the seven hills
saṅkataharaṇa	The destroyer of sorrows
vāsudēva	Son of Vasudeva (Krishna)
ram jinka nam hē	His name is Ram
ayōdhya jinka nam hē	His home is Ayodhya
aisē raghu nandan kō	To the descendant of the Raghu dynasty
hamāra bhi praṇam hē	I, too, offer my prostrations
aise daya sagar kō viṭhalā	To that Ocean of mercy Krishna

VĒṆUGŌPA BĀLĀ NĪ

vēṇugōpa bālā nī
pōrukente cārē
mama mānasam viṭarttān oru
gānamūtiyāṭū
gānamūtiyāṭū

O Cowherd Boy with the flute, please come near me. Dance and sing to allow my mind to blossom.

kāḷiyante phaṇamēṛi ninnoru
celezhum naṭanam āṭu nī
rāma sahitam ōrōgōparottu
vṛndāvana līlakaḷādu nī

Dance gracefully on the hood of Kaliya, the serpent. Dance with Rama and each of the Gopis, the players of Vrindavan.

cūṭi cēlil oru pīli kūntaloṭu
nīla mēgha niṛamārna nī
rādha tannuṭaya rāsakēḷi yatil
mōṭicērnu naṭamāṭu nī

Thou, with the complexion of blue rain clouds, wearing a peacock feather in the hair, join gracefully with Radha in her rasa dance.

VIḶICĀL VIḶI KĒḶKKĀN

viḷicāl viḷi kēḷkkān maṭikkuvaṭentammē
tanichī vanāntarattil vasikkunnu ñān
smaricāl manatāril vasippān varikillē
stutichāl stuti kēḷkkān orukkamillē

Why art Thou hesitating to reply to my call, O Mother? I am left alone in the midst of this forest. Won't Thou come to dwell in my mind when I remember Thee? Art Thou not ready to hear my prayers when I sing Thy glories?

manasinte vipinattil madamenna mṛgarājan
madichu tuḷḷunnenne hanichu tinnān
bramicha mānpēṭa pōl bramichu nilkunnu ñān
tuṇaykkāyi nin mizhikkōṇ onnanakkukillē ammē

In the forest of the mind, pride, the ruttish lion, is roaming around to kill and eat me. Like a perplexed doe, I remain transfixed. Won't Thou cast a sidelong glance to help me?

vidhiyenna svapachante kṣaṇattāl bhuvanattil
virunnuṇṇan iniyenne ayaykkarutē
aviratam aviṭutte padatāril mati cērnu
maruvuvān anugraham aruḷukammē ammē

At the invitation of thankless fate, please do not send me again to Earth for the mundane feast. Kindly bless me, Mother, to remain with my mind incessantly adhering to Thy Feet.

VINĀVILAMBAM

vināvilambam kṛpāvalambam
tarān varū jananī
nirantaram tava kṛpāmṛtam lavam
irannu nilppū ñān

Come, O Mother, to give mercy without any delay! I am always begging for the ambrosia of Your compassion.

bhavāni nin tiru padāmbujam hṛdi
sadā smarikkunnu
parātpare cuṭu bāṣpa kaṇaṅgaḷ
vṛtha pozhikkunnu

O Mother, I am always remembering Your lotus feet in my heart. O Goddess, my eyes simply pour out hot tears!

viṣāda cintaykkadhīnayāyi ñān
nissānayākkarutē
orittu snēham pakarnnu nalkuka
suśānti neṭīṭān

Let me not become worthless by becoming a prey to sad thoughts. In order to have some peace, please give at least one drop of love!

durūha vismayamallō tāvaka
vibhinna bhāvaṅgaḷ
tvadanya cintakaḷ ezhāykilārkkum
nija paramānandam

Your different moods are incomprehensible and at the same time surprising. If somebody has only thoughts of You, he will enjoy supreme bliss.

hṛdāntamammē nitānta bhaktyā
tavāmghṛpatmatte
mukarnnu mōdam viḷangiṭaṭṭe
vilīnamakaṭṭe

May I kiss Your lotus feet with ceaseless devotion within my heart, and thus, O Mother, may I ever enjoy happiness and finally become immersed in You!

VIPHALAMŌ ENNUṬE

viphalamō ennuṭe
manuṣya janmam
vijaya lakṣmī enne anugrahikkû

Is this human life of mine going to waste? If so, O Goddess of Good Fortune, please shower Your blessings on me.

vila keṭṭatō ente
manuṣa janmam eṅkil
vidhi dāyini enne anugrahikkû

Is this human life of mine worth nothing? If so, O Bestower of Final Judgement, please shower Your blessings on me.

azhalāzhīlāññu ñān kēṇiṭunnu ente
manassine kaṛayere
kārnīṭunnu kanivoṭe kaniyillē
tiru darśanam ninte mṛdu bhakti
sudha enikkēkiṭumō

I beseech Thee, I have lost my way in an ocean of sorrow, and my mind is tainted by one impurity after another. Won't You grant me kindly Your divine darshan, and bestow on me the nectar of sweet devotion?

tiru cinta kondente mōhamellām
akalaṭṭe unmattayākkīṭanē
kanivōṭenikkēku prēma bhakti
ninnil layikkunna śuddha bhakti

May all my delusions be wiped out by one movement of Your Supreme Will. May I reach the state of divine intoxication. Kindly grant me pure devotion — the sweet Love that merges in You.

onnē enikkoru nitya śānti atu
nin maṭittoṭṭilām nitya sthānam
ammē tazhukiyuṟakkiyennē
nin maṭittoṭṭilil āṭṭiṭanē

I know just one abode of eternal peace - the cradle of Your lap. O Mother, caress me and rock me to sleep in that sweet cradle of Your lap.

VIRAHATTĪ PAṬARUNNEN

virahattī paṭarunnen hṛdayattil ammē
kanivinde panīniru kuṭayān varillē
tirayunnu ñān dūre maruvunnu ñān ammē
azhalāḷum ātmavin iniyennu śānti

O Mother, the fire of separation from You is spreading everywhere in my heart. Won't You come and sprinkle some fragrant water of compassion? I am far away and wandering in search of You. When will this restless soul find peace?

mana mulla viriyunna naṟu veṇṇilāvil
oru nōkku kaṇi kāṇān uzhaṟun ennuḷḷam
aṇayillayō hṛttil aṇayumbōl nī ārum
paṟayāte taniye ñān aṟiyum mahēśi

My mind is pining for 'Kani' (First darshan on an auspicious day), that is rare like the moonlit night when the jasmin bud blooms. Won't You come closer? When You come closer, my heart will know it, without a word about needing to be spoken, and it is longing for that auspicious first intimation of Your Presence.

azhalinte veyilēttu valayunna hṛdayam
tazhukān nin snēhattin kara tāranaykku
tiriyilla ñān pāta veṭiyilla ñān, ninne
aṟiyānuḷḷati mōham veṭiyilla ñān

Please extend Your hand of love and caress this heart parched by the blistering noon-day heat of worldly sorrows. I will never forsake the path. I will never forsake You. I will never give up the keen hunger to know Thee.

VIŚVAMĀTRU SVABHĀVA

viśvamātru svabhāva muḷkondiṭum
viśvavātsalya dhāmamē kaitozhām
tyāgam tan divya jīvitamākkiya
tyāga mūrttiye kaitozhām kaitozhām

I bow down before the storehouse of universal motherhood who is the embodiment of that. I bow down before that embodiment of self-sacrifice who made Her life itself a sacrifice.

ninte kāruṇyadhāra varṣikkaṇē
nin tiru snēha meṅkalozhukaṇē!
śuddha bhaktiyum nirmmala prēmavum
sīmayatennil nī niṛachīṭanē

Shower Your stream of love upon us and let Your divine love flow through me. May You fill my heart with limitless pure love and faith.

nitya vastu svarūpiṇī sadgurō
sajjanāvana sēvitē nirmalē
satya vastuvilen manam nityavum
magnamākuvān kaitozhām kaitozhām!

O Eternal Master (Satguru), the embodiment of Eternal Truth, O Purity, who is served by good-hearted people, let my mind be immersed in that Eternal Truth. I prostrate before You again and again.

VIṬARUNNA KALIKAYKKU

viṭarunna kalikaykku gatiyentu kāḷikē?
kozhiyunna pūvinnu gatiyentu māyikē?
oḷichintum minnalin gatiyentu kāḷikē?
eriyunna citayuṭe kathayentennambikē?

O Kalike, what is the fate of a blooming bud? O Enchantress, what is the fate of a withering flower? O Kalike, what is the fate of light shining as lightning? O my Mother, what is the story of a burning funeral pyre?

gatiyentu kathayentu vivasanām śiśuvinu
jananī nī kanivenye maruvukilambikē?
karayunna paitalin svaramamba kēḷkkayikil
karayumī jīvante gatiyentennambikē?

O Mother, what is the fate and destiny of this destitute child if You remain merciless? If Mother is not heeding the wails of Her crying child, what is the course left for this weeping soul?

ceḷipatti kaṭiyēttu piṭayumī kuññine
ariya mātāvallativitāru nōkkuvān?
karatāril kōri nin śiśuvine puṇaraykil
vazhiyeṅgu teḷiveṅgu tunayeṅgu kāḷikē?

Who else is there to look after this fluttering child, who is filth-covered and bitten, except You, the dearest Mother? If You are not embracing Your child by taking it in Your hands, where is the way, where is the proof (of Your love), where is the assistance, O Kalike?

ihamamma paramamma sakalatum nīyamma
madhurita vatsalyattikavāṇu nīyamma
śaraṇam enikkamma nī tanne nī tanne
ninavilla ninne viṭṭonnumennambikē!

This world is Mother, the other world also is Mother, everything else is Mother. O Mother, You are the embodiment of sweet tenderness. You alone are my sole refuge. O Mother, I can't live without You!

VIṬHALĀ VIṬHALĀ

viṭhalā viṭhalā viṭhalā [5]
viṭhalā viṭhalā viṭhalā
ō mātā viṭhalā pāṇḍurangā
jai jai viṭhalā viṭhalā viṭhalā
jai jai viṭhalā viṭhalā viṭhalā

---

[5] Vithala specifically refers to Krishna's (Vishnu) form as Panduranga in Pandaripur near Poona

Vishnu, Vishnu, Vishnu. O Mother (Lakshmi) and the Lord Panduranga. Victory, victory to Vishnu

VṚNDĀVANA KĒ SUNDARA

vṛndāvana kē sundara bālā
mañjuḷa hāsa yutā
sundara vadanā vandita caraṇā
manda gamana gōpāl

O handsome Youth from Vrindavan, O Gopal with a lovely face and charming smile, who walks slowly with feet worthy of worship!

mōru mukuṭa sir kañjan nayana
cañjala kuṇḍal kān
mangala mūrtti kē sankh gālē mē
rājat kaustubh hār

The peacock feather on Your crown, the collyrium in Your eyes, the shimmering earrings hanging from Your ears, the garland of the "Kaustubha" jewel shining upon Your conch-shaped neck — all these make Thy auspicious form even more enchanting to behold.

candana ur mē vana mālā hē
pītāmbar kaṭi mē
paiñjani rañjit mañju padom mē
añjali baddh praṇām
kṛṣṇā añjali baddh praṇām
mērē añjali baddh praṇām

There is the garland of forest flowers hanging upon Your sandal-fragranced body, and the yellow raiment around Your waist. Oh Krishna, I offer my salutations with folded palms at Your feet bedecked with tinkling anklets.

VṚNDĀVANATTILE RĀDHA

vṛndāvanattile rādha
kaṇṇante priya sakhi rādha
kaṇṇante vēṇuvāyi tīrnnu avaḷ
kaṇṇante śvāsamāyi tīrnnu rādha rādha

Radha of Vrindavan, Radha who is the dearest friend of Kanna, became Kanna's flute! Indeed, she became Kanna's life-breath!

niṛabhakti lahariyil rādha - avaḷ
kaṇṇanumāyi nṛttamāṭi
kaṇṇante mayilppīliyāyī - avaḷ
kaṇṇante kaṇṇayi tīrnnu rādha rādha

Radha, in devotional ecstasy, danced with Krishna. She became Kanna's peacock feather! She indeed became Kanna's eyes!

kaṇṇante mānasa ṛāni - avaḷ
prēmattin paryāyamāyi
kannanilāzhnavaḷ cērnu - prēma
sāgaramāyaval tīrnnu rādha rādha

She is the queen of Kanna's mind. She became the synonym of love. Immersing and becoming one with Kanna, she became an ocean of love!

YADUPATI MANAHARI

yadupati manahari nirupama guṇamayi
rādhē jaya jaya navarasikē
hari virahiṇi vraja vipina vihāriṇi
surajana nata pada kamalayutē

mṛdumṛdu hasitamukhi manahāriṇi
rāsavasōjjvala kāntimayi
madhuripu hṛdaya vilāsini mōhini
manalaya kāriṇi jaya rādhē

rādhē śyām rādhē śyām
rādhē śyām śyām śyām rādhē śyām
navanava madhumaya rāgavinōdini
mṛdupada naṭana vilāsamayī
vrajavana kuñja nivāsini rāgiṇi
rāsa rāsēśvari jaya rādhē!
rādhē śyām rādhē śyām

vrajaramaṇī kula mauli manōhari
yugala manōhara naṭanaratē
murali manōhara vadana vilōkini
vidhi śiva vandita caraṇayugē
rādhē śyām rādhē śyām

yadupati	The Lord of the Yadu dynasty
manahari	The destroyer of the mind
nirupama guṇamayi	One who has incomparable qualities
navarasikē	One who enjoys the nine types of devotion
hari virahiṇi	Separated from Lord Hari

vrajavipinaviharini	One who sports in the Vraja forests
surajana nata pada kamalayutē	Whose lotus feet are worshipped by the Devas
mṛdumṛdu hasitamukhī	Whose face is lit up with a sweet smile
manahāriṇi	The conqueror of the mind
rasarasōjvala kāntimayi	One who dances brilliantly in the festive dance of the cowherds
madhuripu hṛdayavilāsini	Who sports in the heart of the destroyer of the demon madhu
mōhini	Charming
manalayakāriṇi	Who causes tranquillity of mind
rādhe	Beloved of Krishna.
śyām	Dark colored Krishna.
navanava madhumayaraga vinōdini	One who sports with ever new nectarian love
mṛdupadanatana vilāsamayi	One who dances with soft steps
vrajavana kuñjanivāsini	One who lives in the groves of the Vraja forest
rāgini	The passionate one
vrajaramani kula mauli	The crown among all Vraja gopis
yugalamanōhara naṭanaratē	One who dances beautifully with Krishna
muralimanōhara vadanavilōkini	Who watches the face of the charming flute player
vidhi śiva vandita caraṇayugē	Whose feet are worshipped by Brahma and Shiva

Index of Bhajans Volume 2

www.ingramcontent.com/pod-product-compliance
Lightning Source LLC
LaVergne TN
LVHW051541080426
835510LV00020B/2811